WHY CHILDREN MISBEHAVE

Bruce Narramore

WHY CHILDREN MISBEHAVE

ZONDERVAN
PUBLISHING HOUSE   OF THE ZONDERVAN CORPORATION
GRAND RAPIDS, MICHIGAN 49506

Illustrations by Diane Head

WHY CHILDREN MISBEHAVE
Copyright © 1980 by The Zondervan Corporation

Library of Congress Cataloging in Publication Data

Narramore, Bruce.
    Why children misbehave.

    1. Parenting.   2. Child psychology.   I. Title.
HQ755.8.N372   649'.1   80-24760
ISBN 0-310-30360-5

Unless otherwise indicated, Scripture quotations are from The Holy Bible, The New International Version, copyright © 1978 by the New York International Bible Society. Used by permission.

Printed in the United States of America

Contents

Part 1

PREVENTIVE PARENTING

Chapter 1

PARENTING CAN BE POSITIVE

If you are like most parents, you occasionally have "one of those days." As soon as you get up in the morning—or sometimes even before—things begin to fall apart. Something crashes to the floor in the kitchen. One of your children is crying, and the other is griping or teasing or in some kind of trouble. From this beginning the situation gets progressively worse. If you have young children, there is constant fussing, whining, and crying. If you have teen-agers, they are repeatedly at each other's throat. By the end of the day you feel ready for a rest home—or at least a long vacation! If you pause to reflect on the day's activities you probably decide that no two or three normal children could cause so much trouble unless they had stayed up late the night before plotting the whole thing! When this happens, most of us tend to respond with our own forms of misbehavior. We become cross, irritable, and stubborn. We lose our tempers and speak harshly and with disrespect. We may even yell and chase everyone else out of the house or into their rooms! These are difficult times, because it is never easy to keep our cool in the middle of chaos. Some days we just have "more than we can take."

9

Too Little Too Late

If these occasional chaotic days were our only problems, most of us could cope fairly well. We could steel ourselves for these periodical battles and comfort ourselves with the knowledge that our really bad times are few and far between. Unfortunately most of us spend far too much of our in-between time refereeing, policing, and disciplining our chil-

dren for less critical but nevertheless very upsetting activities. We spend hours threatening, correcting, or consoling. We constantly have to drop what we are doing and run to our children's sides to settle a squabble or to instruct, correct, or discipline. At mealtimes we repeatedly tell them to "say please," "clean your plate," or "eat at least one bite of everything." As our offspring grow older we "remind" them to clean their rooms, to take out the trash, or to do their homework.

Day after day and week after week we are spending countless hours telling, correcting, or instructing our children *after* they have gotten into trouble. Gradually and almost imperceptibly, parenting becomes a hassle. Because we are so busy correcting our children, we find ourselves spending less and less time just having fun together or enjoying each other's company.

I call this a "fire engine approach" to parenting. We try to put out one fire after another—but always *after* trouble has begun. This approach is more concerned with correction than prevention, and our roles are more like policemen than leaders and teachers. Gradually our vision of a happy, fulfilling family life grows tarnished under the onslaught of daily reality. Periodically we step back long enough to vow to do better or to improve the situation somehow; but before long we are right back in the old negative pattern.

An Ounce of Prevention

The Bible says, "Children are a gift from God; they are his reward. Children born to a young man are like sharp arrows to defend him. Happy is the man who has his quiver full of them" (Ps. 127:3–4 LIVING BIBLE). Unfortunately many parents today have lost sight of the fact that children are a gift of God and that they should bring joy, not conflict, to our homes. We have fallen into the trap of seeing children as objects or as obstacles that interfere with our freedom and fulfillment. Sometimes we even resent their presence and wish we had an empty quiver!

This doesn't have to be. There is an alternative approach to parenting that focuses more on the fun times we can have together than it does on problems and misunderstandings. It focuses on positive planning and training that nips problems in the bud rather than waiting for warfare to break out. And it focuses on increasing family unity and understanding instead of constant nagging, bickering, and fighting.

I believe a positive parenting experience is within the reach of every family. It isn't always easy, and solutions don't come overnight. But with a little understanding of our children's needs—and our own—we can begin to solve many problems and move toward an enriching, positive experience together. A positive approach to parenting can help recapture that sense of awe and love and unity we had when our children were first born. And it can help restore a good measure of peace and happiness around the place called home.

I don't mean that all our family problems can be solved and we will never have another hassle with our children. As long as we are human we will "have our days." But we can learn to avoid many problems, to solve others positively, and to stimulate an atmosphere of cooperation and mutual enjoyment. We can find ways of relating to our children that remove a great deal of punishment and pressure. As we do, we open up ourselves and our children to new and positive experiences.

This is one of my greatest rewards in our own family. We have our share of problems, but we have learned to handle most of them constructively. We have made enough progress that we really do enjoy each other. I love to come home and spend time with Dickie and Debbie. Kathy and I look forward to vacations—not just to "get away," but to be together with the family. And we continually find fun and rewarding things to do together. The keys to this are an understanding of ourselves and our children, some positive planning and prevention, and a good plan for constructive discipline.

In the next chapter we will look at some of the needs we have as parents and some of the struggles we face. Before we launch into ways of influencing our children, we need to realize that we have needs and rights of our own. We do not have to sacrifice our fulfillment in life by enslaving ourselves to our children for twenty years. If we try to deny these needs or become martyr parents who ignore our needs in order to focus exclusively on our children's, we are headed for trouble. We do ourselves, our spouses, and our children a great disservice. In chapter 3 we will look at why children reared in the same home can be so different and why some children are more difficult to parent than others.

Parts 2 and 3 discuss the major causes of our children's misbehavior. We will see that all children (and adults, for that matter) have several basic emotional needs. If these needs are met, our children tend to get along quite well. But if they are not, some predictable problems are likely to occur.

The goal of these chapters is to help us identify the causes for our children's problems so we can learn to parent preventively—that is, to take steps to solve our children's problems *before* they erupt into disturbing misbehavior. In brief, the purpose of this book is to help us identify our children's needs and develop a plan for meeting them.

To help you apply the concepts of *Why Children Misbehave* I have also written a workbook called *The Power of Positive Parenting*. That book is designed for study groups or your individual use. It takes each of the reasons for misbehavior we discuss here and helps you see how they may be operating in your family and what you can do about them. As you read this book you may want to get a copy of *The Power of Positive Parenting* and work through some of the specific problems or hassles your children are facing in a step-by-step way. Once we really understand why our children are acting and feeling as they do, it is not too difficult to head off much misbehavior at the pass and develop a plan of positive parenting.

Chapter 2

PARENTS HAVE RIGHTS TOO!

Most books on rearing children contain a lot of good advice on meeting children's needs. They help us understand our children's need for love and limits and offer practical ways of guiding children to maturity with a minimum of psychic damage. This advice and understanding can be very helpful. In fact, a significant portion of this book is written for that very purpose. But if we aren't careful, we can focus so intently on our children's needs that we forget that parents are people too. We have our own needs, our own feelings, our own desires, and our own responsibilities. We are not simply our children's guardians. We existed as individuals and couples before our children were born and will continue to do so long after they leave the nest.

Consequently, before looking at our responsibilities to our children, let's take a few minutes to look at our responsibilities to ourselves and our spouses. If we are unable to meet our own needs, it will be impossible for us to find fulfillment in our roles as parents—and both we and our children will suffer for it. One of the saddest situations I encounter as a psychologist is that of a parent (usually a mother) who has totally thrown her life into her children only to wake up in her forties with the children gone, a sterile marriage, and no sense of who she is as a person. She has been so busy trying to be a good parent that she has lost sight of the fact that she is a person too! Let's look, then, at a few of our own rights and needs.

Our Need for Time

One of the greatest frustrations mothers of young children face is the lack of time alone. Caring for even one child is a big responsibility and a time-consuming task. But if we happen to have two or three preschool children, we can really encounter a problem. Where, in the middle of all of our responsibilities, do we find any time alone? How can we gain even a few minutes of peace and quiet? And how can we get out of the house and away from the children without feeling guilty for abandoning them? In short, how can we be both a person and a parent? As Julie, the frustrated mother of a seven-month-old baby told me, "I seem to spend all day taking care of one end or the other! There is never time for me!"

When I asked a group of parents to discuss the most frustrating problem they faced, one mother replied, "My biggest frustration was when Penny was small and so demanding. Every time I turned around she thought she needed something. Sometimes I just felt like stuffing her under the bed or tossing her out the window—not to hurt her, but just to make her shut up!"

These mothers expressed feelings many parents would hesitate to admit. But they are entirely normal. Everyone has a legitimate need for time alone, and none should have to apologize for it. It is impossible to meet our own needs fully if we spend twenty-four hours a day assuming responsibility for our offspring.

In our society it is usually the mother who encounters this particular conflict. Since men generally work outside the home, they have a convenient escape from the ongoing demands of young children! If you are feeling these frustrations, it would be very good to stop now and have a long talk with your husband. Explain your need for a little time and space. A sensitive husband will understand. If he doesn't, ask him to change places with you for several days or a week. I am sure he will see your point of view long before the time is up!

While discussing your needs with your spouse, be honest with your feelings. Let him know you "love the kids but sometimes they get on my nerves." Let him know you aren't ready to run off and abandon the family, but at times you need to be alone. And let him know you still need time with your friends. Then plan with your husband how it can be done.

Can your husband relieve you of some of the responsibilities? Do you have grandparents nearby who can help? Is there a baby-sitting co-op you can join? Is one of the children ready for nursery school? Can you hire a baby sitter a couple of mornings a week? Or would a housekeeper coming in for a half-day each week improve the situation? These are just a few of the many possibilities for making a little time for yourself.

Once you decide how to provide the time, you can decide how to spend it. Would you like just to be left alone? Do you need some time to shop? Would you enjoy a Bible study group or a weekly tennis match? Or would you even like a part-time job? While there are some real difficulties in trying to hold down a job and be a responsible parent, some women find a relief and a fulfillment in their work that makes them better mothers. If this is true of you, don't be afraid to consider the possibility. It is one way of getting relief from some really difficult responsibilities and having a bit more time just for yourself. And when you feel better about yourself, you will do better with your children. A tense, bored, overworked, or stifled woman is in no condition to be a happy parent!

You and Your Spouse

Close on the heels of our need for time alone is the need for time with our mate. God created marriage before He created children, and we must not forget that marriage is the basic institution of society. It is likely that we were married for a significant period of time before we became parents, and if we follow the statistical average, we will have a full three decades of married life after our children reach adulthood and leave home.

We must not assume we can take a twenty-year vacation from working on our marriage while we are rearing children. All of us need regular communication. If we don't have these times with our mate, tensions begin to build and problems surface. Husbands can easily feel left out when wives spend most of their time with the children, and wives can feel unloved when husbands fail to make a habit of finding time to be together without the children.

Carol, the mother of a baby girl, described her experience as a parent and a marriage partner. She wrote:

> I had no idea babies could be so time-consuming. I felt like a stranger to my husband because there just was no time for us to be alone. Keith wasn't the kind to get involved with feeding, bathing, or that kind of thing, so I began to put all of my energy into Kimberly.
> This caused us to drift apart even more and I found myself loving and hating Kimberly at the same time. One day I had a talk with a good friend and realized what was happening. Kimberly was becoming the center of my attention, and Keith was being pushed aside.

Carol's experience is common. Fortunately she realized she was falling into a trap and began to break out. She talked the problem over with her husband, and they found ways of meeting both their needs and those of their young daughter.

A weekly evening out, a regular time together after the children are in bed, and an occasional weekend away from home can all help keep our marriages alive and make us better persons and better parents. When our children are old enough to sleep over at a friend's home, arrange for them to be out for a night or two. Some couples take turns keeping

each other's children for a weekend. This frees them up for a weekend trip, a night at a fine hotel, or just a quiet evening together at home.

The possibilities are endless, and the principle is simple. When we become parents we do not cease to be partners. If we are going to enjoy a happy family life, we must give attention to our own needs and the needs of our mates as well as those of our children.

Guilt-free Parenting

There are no perfect parents. No matter how good our intentions and no matter how hard we try, we are all going to make mistakes in rearing children. Some mistakes are small and of little consequence; others are more serious and have lasting negative results. But whatever the nature of our limitations as parents, we all tend to feel guilty for our failures. This is entirely normal and to be expected. But sometimes our guilt feelings compound our problems. We read books and attend lectures on rearing children, and every time we do, we see a few more things we are doing wrong. Instead of getting help we just get burdened under a heavier load of guilt. And the guiltier we feel, the more frustrated we are with the children. Little things upset us more. Their public misbehavior irritates us more. And in general we are all a bit more miserable. This doesn't have to be. There is a way of honestly looking at our parenting strengths and weaknessess without blaming either ourselves or our mates. We can develop an attitude toward ourselves and our children that focuses on the positive and helps to overcome the tendency to over-emphasize our mistakes and failures.

The starting place for guilt-free parenting is facing the fact that we are human. There are no perfect parents. There never have been, and there never will be! As members of the human race we should never expect perfection from ourselves. The best we can expect is that we are growing people and growing parents. If we are honest about our weaknesses and failures and giving attention to them, we will gradually begin to change. In fact, the Greek word translated "perfect" in some versions of the New Testament was actually used in Christ's day to refer to maturity. It communicated the sense of a fully developed or ripe fruit—one that had gone through its seasons and reached a certain level of maturity.

Some of us expect to be "instant parents." One reason why God planned the average pregnancy to take nine months is to give the potential parents time to start adapting. And one reason children take the better part of two decades to reach maturity is that both parents and children need time to learn to accept themselves as they really are. When Jesus Christ died on the cross to pay for our sins, He didn't ask us to be anything we are not. He took us as we are.

One of the greatest lessons in life is the knowledge that we can accept ourselves the way we are. We can accept ourselves with our tempers, our periods of depression, our busy schedules, our moments of frustration, and our occasional desires to "get away from it all." No matter what our weaknesses and failures may be, we will never really begin to grow until we give up our self-rejection and learn to take ourselves the way we are.

Closely related to the ability to accept ourselves the way we are is the ability to forgive ourselves. When Christ died on the cross, He paid the penalty for our sins. Romans 8:1 says, "There is therefore now no condemnation to them that are in Christ Jesus." This means that the moment people place their faith in Jesus Christ, their sins are totally forgiven and they become acceptable to God. From that moment on, God holds no grudges. He both forgives and forgets our sins—and expects us to do the same. If God does not condemn us, we have no need to condemn ouselves. Nowhere in the entire New Testament is the Christian commanded to feel guilty. God expects us to be honest about our failures and to acknowledge our sins; but He never asks us to "get on our case" or condemn ourselves for our weaknesses or failures. Instead, He wants us to focus on the fact that we are forgiven so we can forget the past and move on to a more successful future.

If you find yourself repeatedly giving yourself a hard time about not being the perfect parent, you may want to take time to read a little more about the Christian's freedom from guilt. A few years ago a friend and I wrote a book by that title and just recently a mother told me she felt it was an excellent introduction to parenting.[1] "Even though that book has absolutely nothing on how to parent," she said, "it gave me an attitude I needed. It let me see how I could accept myself and get over my tendency to blame myself so I could start to focus on the positive."

The Right to Guide Our Children

The wave of permissiveness that has swept this country since the early 1940s has tended to obscure the fact that parents have the right to guide and direct their children's lives.

---

[1]Bruce Narramore and Bill Counts, *Freedom From Guilt* (Irvine, Calif.: Harvest House, 1974).

Without being tyrants or slavemasters, we have both the right and responsibility to guide and train our children. This includes the right to see that they do not do some things they would like to do and that they do some things they would rather not!

To understand this right, we need to look briefly at four styles of parenting. These four styles are actually ways of leading or governing a family. They range from the extreme permissiveness propounded by some non-Christian, humanistic writers to a dogmatic authoritarianism that is sometimes suggested by misguided Christian writers.

Authoritarian Parents

The authoritarian parent is the absolute and unquestioned authority in the family. He or she assumes the right not only to guide and direct the children, but also to try to shape them—by whatever means are necessary—into what he or she thinks they should become. This parent believes children are basically rebellious and sinful: left to their own devices, the children will get into nothing but trouble. Children will not naturally grow and develop positive characteristics, so they need a great deal of parental discipline.

With this view of the nature of children, authoritarian parents are quick to tell their children what to do. They set many limits and restrictions and do not give their children much voice in decisions affecting the family. When it is time for vacation, these parents make their own decisions and inform the children where they will be going. If they move to a new neighborhood, the parents decide where they will live and attend church and then inform the children. When it is time to eat, these parents decide what foods to prepare, and the children are to eat it. There is no discussion and very little soliciting of children's wishes, desires, or preferences. The parents are in control.

When it comes to discipline, authoritarian parents rely heavily on physical correction. They take little time to discuss

or reason with their children because children are expected to "do what they are told." Obedience is the parents' major goal. They believe that if children can only be taught to obey, everything else will fall into place. They take the Bible's emphasis on obedience of children as the only—or at least the major—task of parental training, and they use force to see that obedience is learned. Here is one example of how an author following an authoritarian approach suggests handling a fifteen-year-old boy who "forgot" to rake the lawn and had been playing basketball instead:

> You know, son, even though you have been careless with my orders, I can't be careless with God's orders. I don't dare. I have to be careful when God gives me something to do. I'm going to punish you, because God's Word expects me to. However, it is not for deliberate disobedience. I take your word for it that you forgot. It's a serious thing to be careless with an order given you by someone who has both the power and the right to punish you. I have the power and I am going to use it. One day you will stand before God who has the power to punish you eternally if you are careless with His orders. Excuses don't count with God. I can't accept them either. Do you understand what I am saying, son? I don't want you growing up thinking excuses can be substituted for obedience![2]

And after the son acknowledges he knows what the father is saying, the father continues: "That's right. So I am going to use this strap on you. It will hurt, but not nearly so much as if you had deliberately disobeyed me. God deals with us the same way. He accepts our good intentions, but He does not overlook our disobedience. We have to suffer the consequences of our carelessness with His orders."

This is an extreme form of authoritarianism and one that I suspect few parents would even consider. But it does point out several of the basic aspects of authoritarian parenting. Notice the stress on obedience: the entire emphasis is on making sure the son learns to obey. And notice the parents' emphasis on power: the father lets his son know he has greater power and intends to use it. Then notice the emphasis on physical spanking! Of all the possible means of correcting a teen-ager for not raking the lawn, this father suggests corporal punishment. No thought is given to a logical consequence

---

[2]C. S. Lovett, *What's a Parent to Do?* (Baldwin Park, Calif.: Personal Christianity, 1971), p. 92.

such as "no raking, no basketball." And no thought is given to a consequence such as no television until the leaves are raked. The only discipline suggested is a spanking—and this for a fifteen-year-old boy who the father admits was not deliberately disobeying! Imagine what could happen if the son disobeyed on purpose!

Few of us go to this extreme. But many of us operate on very similar assumptions. We assume children are basically sinful and rebellious. We assume they should "be seen and not heard." We assume parents have the right to make all the family's decisions. We assume our primary task as parents is to make sure our children are obedient. And we assume physical power is the best way of teaching our offspring to be obedient. When they disobey or refuse to cooperate, we become angry and upset. *We* are the parents, we think. What right do *they* have to disobey us? But if our *children* become angry with *us*, we do not allow it. We think, "Children have no right to speak to me that way! I can get mad and shout at them if I wish because I am the parent. But they are only children and they must treat me with respect!" Respect, in other words, is a one-way street. Our children must not get angry with us but must communicate respect; but we have the right to get angry and upset with them.

During the first decade or so of our children's lives, we may be able to get by with some authoritarian methods. As long as they are young, they really cannot fight back too strenuously —at least by overt, aggressive acts. Consequently we may not see too many negative efforts of our power-oriented methods. Even if our children become somewhat overly negativistic, we assume it is because they are stubborn or negative. We don't stop to consider that their negativism may be a reaction to our excessive control. And even if they become a bit withdrawn, fearful, or overly anxious, we just assume they were born that way. We don't stop to ask ourselves if their shyness, anxiety, or fear may be a reaction to our temper outbursts, our rigid controls, or our power-oriented method of relating.

The problems may not begin to become obvious until adolescence or even early adulthood. It is then, under the sway of feelings of resentment that have been growing beneath the surface for years, that the negative influence of our authoritarian methods begins to really show. Sometimes it is expressed in overt rebellion. Sometimes it comes out in persistent arguing, sassing, and negativism toward us and all we stand for. Sometimes it appears in efforts to escape into drugs, alcohol, or promiscuous sex. And sometimes it emerges in feelings of serious depression, worry, and anxiety. But whatever its exact nature, we can expect authoritarian parenting eventually to take its toll. In failing to place as much value on our children's rights as we do our own, we program them for some form of emotional or spiritual maladjustment.

Permissive Parents

The permissive parent is at the opposite end of the continuum. He or she is not particularly concerned about obedience. The primary goal is providing children with an environment that is conducive to the natural unfolding of their true selves. The philosophy underlying this approach to rearing children is that human nature is essentially good or, at worst, neutral. Since children are viewed as essentially good rather than evil, the emphasis is on self-expression, self-direction, and self-determination. There is little or no place for the parent to discipline or direct, because it is assumed that children naturally have the potential to make their own decisions. Rousseau, probably the most notable forerunner of the modern permissive movement, wrote that children "should never act from obedience but from necessity. For this reason, the words 'obey' and 'command' must be banished from his vocabulary, still more the words 'duty' and 'obligation.'" And Thomas Gordon, founder of the popular Parent Effectiveness Training program, says, "The stubborn persis-

"We want him to feel free to express himself."

tence of the idea that parents must and should use authority in dealing with children has, in my opinion, prevented for centuries any significant change or improvement in the way children are raised by parents and treated as adults."[3]

These comments point to the major features of permissive approaches to parenting. Children are born essentially good. They should be allowed full self-direction. And parents should never use their authority over their children.

This optimistic approach to child rearing has several serious limitations. To begin with, the Bible makes it clear that children are not born essentially good. Although they are created in God's image and have all sorts of capabilities and potential, they are born with sinful and rebellious tendencies. The Bible also tells us that children are to obey their parents (Eph. 6:1). Because of both their immaturity and their sinful bent, children have a definite need for parental discipline, guidance, and correction. Loving discipline helps children learn to curb negative behavior. It also instills a sense of security and helps build a positive sense of self-esteem. Permissiveness undermines both of these much-needed personality characteristics.

"Permissitarian" Parents

In the same way that few of us attempt to rear our children by strictly authoritarian practices, so also few of us are totally permissive. Most of us, however, are permissive in many respects. In fact, probably the most common style of parenting might be called the "permissitarian." That is, we tend to vacillate between permissiveness and authoritarianism. When our children first misbehave, we ignore it. If they are very young, we might even laugh and think "it's cute." But as they grow a little older or when we are a bit uptight, we suddenly change our tune. We *ask* them to cease and desist. Then we *tell* them. And when that fails, we become very angry and

---

[3]Thomas Gordon, *Parent Effectiveness Training: The Tested New Way to Raise Responsible Children* (New York: McKay, 1970), p. 164.

resort to threatening, yelling, or some form of physical punishment or pressure.

Following this mixed approach, we may also vacillate between trusting our children's own decisions and forcing ours on them. We tell them, "Do whatever you think is best, honey." Then we add, "But are you sure that's the right thing?" What we are really saying is, "I trust you, honey, but . . ." And everything that comes after the little three-letter word says we really don't trust the children at all. We are trying to communicate trust and regard, but our own anxiety pushes us to immediately question our children's abilities to make their own decisions.

"Permissitarian" parents also vacillate between seeing children as good and seeing them as evil. Sometimes they praise their children to the hilt; they are proud of them and let them know it. Other times they are completely upset by the children's attitudes and actions. They turn on the children in anger and frustration and ask, "What's the matter with you, anyway? Can't you ever do anything right?"

"Permissitarian" parents, in other words, alternate between giving children the right of self-determination and handling that themselves. They alternate between teaching the children obedience and letting them get by without carrying out their chores or household responsibilities. They alternate between lovingly and sensitively relating to their children and responding to them in anger and frustration.

Biblical Parents

The biblical perspective on family leadership avoids the weaknesses of all three approaches I have described. I call the biblical concept "loving authority." It sees children as neither basically sinful nor essentially good. It sees them first of all as individuals created in the image of God. Because we see children as creations of God, we will treat them with utmost respect. We realize children have many fine abilities, potentialities, and possibilities. We realize they have intelligence of their own. And we realize they have a moral nature. Consequently we relate to them with an awareness of all these strengths and possiblities. But the Bible makes it clear that children are also born with a sinful bent or tendency (Ps. 58:3; Isa. 53:6). This means they must be guided, corrected, and disciplined. A biblical proverb tells us, "The rod of correction imparts wisdom, but a child left to itself disgraces his mother" (Prov. 29:15).

Having some features in common with both authoritarianism and permissiveness, the biblical model of family government combines the best of both in a consistent manner. It does not alternate between one and the other; rather, it drops out the undesirable elements in each. In common with the permissive perspective, the biblical model of parenting places a strong emphasis on children's rights to regard and respect. Instead of being based on humanistic presuppositions, however, this respect is rooted in the fact that all children are bearers of the image of God. Growing out of this same truth is a commitment to be sensitive to children's rights, needs, and interests. The Bible pictures children as extremely important and worthy of respect and sensitive treatment.

In common with authoritarian parenting, on the other hand, the biblical approach acknowledges that children need discipline and correction. Yet, the biblical concept of discipline is quite different from authoritarianism. Biblical authority is a loving authority carried out from a position of parental security. In it we lovingly exercise our authority instead of fighting to win or prove it.

Biblical parenting acknowledges the rights of both parents and children. We can summarize these mutual rights like this:

Parent rights:

    1. A deep sense of personal self-regard and self-respect
    2. A loving and enjoyable home atmosphere
    3. A fulfilling marriage

4. The exercise of leadership and authority in relation to children
5. The setting of sensitive limits and guidelines for children's behavior
6. Treatment with respect and as a worthwhile person

Child rights:

1. A loving home environment where parents are committed to meet physical, spiritual, and emotional needs
2. A deep sense of personal self-regard and self-respect
3. Treatment with respect as a worthwhile person
4. A voice and participation in the family decision-making process
5. Training and instruction according to biblical principles

Chapter 3

YOUR CHILD IS DIFFERENT

If you have read many books on parenting you may have come to the conclusion that all of your children's problems are due to your failures as a parent. Indeed, this is exactly what many, many parents are told. Under the influence of the belief that children are essentially the product of their environment, educators and psychologists have spent much of the past three or four decades trying to convince us that all our children's psychic conflicts can be traced directly to problems in the parent-child relationship.

John B. Watson, the father of modern-day behaviorism, made this fantastic claim:

> Give me a dozen healthy infants, well-formed, and my own specified world to bring them up in, and I'll guarantee to take any one at random and train him to become any type of specialist I might select—doctor, lawyer, artist, merchant, chief, and yes, even beggarman and thief, regardless of his talents, penchants, abilities, vocations, and race of his ancestors.[1]

---

[1]J. B. Watson, *Behaviorism* (New York: W. W. Norton, 1924).

While it is obvious that our relationships with our children are of utmost importance, the belief that parents can perfectly shape a child in any way they wish and that all problems can be blamed on parents has caused a great deal of misunderstanding and needless guilt. It is simply not true that all problems are caused by parents. The Bible, psychological research, and the common experience of almost all parents make it clear that a child's constitutional makeup, his social environment, and his freedom of choice all play important roles in the formation of personality.

Every child comes into this world with a unique style of living, acting, and reacting. Let us think of our own children. If we have more than one, the chances are they were very different from one another from the day we brought them home from the hospital. One of them was a relatively peaceful child; he fit nicely into our arms, seemed to enjoy being held, and before long fell into a happy routine of eating and sleeping. As he grew older he continued to be an easy child to raise. He slept soundly, was generally happy and easy to please, and showed a good bit of flexibility.

Another child of ours may have been totally different. Right from the start he was more active and fidgety. He didn't fit quite as comfortably into our arms. His eating and sleeping patterns were fussy and erratic. While our first child could sleep through an earthquake, we couldn't tiptoe into the second one's room without waking him up. We tried our best to be sensitive to his needs and be cool, calm, and collected— but no matter what we tried, he was different. Little things upset him. He was more active than his older brother. He wore his feelings on his sleeve. He experienced things strongly, and he wants what he wants when he wants it.

No matter how similarly we treat these children, they are going to be different. And no matter how perfect as parents we may be, there is every likelihood that we will have more struggles with the second child because of his basic personality style or temperament.

The Easy Child

Recently Alexander Thomas and Stella Chess, two child psychiatrists, completed a twenty-year study of the temperament and development of a large number of children.[2] The

children in this research were studied from infancy through adolescence to determine the effect of temperament on personality development and to see how a child's basic temperament interacts with environmental influences to shape his or her later adjustment.

After rating each child in nine different dimensions of temperament, the researchers were able to group the children into three general categories.[3] One group was labeled "the Easy Child." Children in this group tended to adapt well to new situations, develop regular eating and sleeping schedules, have a positive approach to new situations, be rather predictable or consistent, meet new people with a smile, and handle frustration rather well. Easy Children are a joy to any parents who are fortunate enough to have them. They are adaptable rather than demanding, and they can make any parent look great! Because they are not high-strung, we are able to relax and take life easier. There is less urge to threaten, pressure, or worry about these children.

---

[2]Alexander Thomas and Stella Chess, *Temperament and Development* (New York: Brunner-Mazel, 1977).

[3]The nine dimensions were activity level, rhythmicity, approach or withdrawal, adaptability, threshold of responsiveness, intensity of reaction, quality of mood, distractability and attention span, and persistence.

And because we worry less, we feel better about ourselves and our roles. It is easier for us to accept ourselves, and it is easier to love our children.

The Slow-to-Warm-Up Child

Thomas and Chess labeled their second group of children "the Slow-to-Warm-Up Child." Children in this group generally had a mildly negative response to anything or anyone new. In contrast to Easy Children, these children met strangers with hesitancy or mild negativism. They also approached new foods, new activities, and new experiences hesitantly. If they were handled carefully and given the opportunity, however, these children gradually warmed up and learned to relate well.

The Difficult Child

The third group was called "the Difficult Child." Children in this group were almost the opposite of the Easy Children. They tended to withdraw or respond negatively to all new situations, they were irregular and unpredictable, they had intense moods (which were often negative), their eating and sleeping habits were irregular, and they frequently laughed or cried loudly. Children like this are difficult for us to parent, of course. They do not tend to draw warm-fuzzy responses from us, because they do not fit nicely into our routine. They do not charm strangers at the market the way Easy Children do, and they don't even take the quiet, hesitant approach of the Slow-to-Warm-Up Children. Instead, they make their presence known in ways that are often upsetting. They cry, fuss, fight, and in scores of ways refuse to adapt.

The poor adaptability of the Difficult Child tends to stir up anger, frustration, and anxiety on the part of parents. We become irritated because these children "won't cooperate." They upset our routine and are continually making life difficult. They also cause us a great deal of anxiety because we wonder what is wrong. And they provoke guilt because we assume we are somehow to blame for their maladaptive style.

Handling Different Types of Children

We don't have to be psychologists to realize that these three types of children call for very different skills and sensitivities on the part of parents. What is good for one of these children will not necessarily be good for the other. The Easy Child, for example, may end up having problems just because he is so easy to raise. Placed in a family with a Difficult Child, the Easy Child can become lost in the cracks. His more aggressive, active, or negativistic brother is more likely to become the center of parental attention because his antics stir greater parental concern. Consequently parents of Easy Children have to be especially sensitive to the needs for encour-

agement, attention, and support. Slow-to-Warm-Up Children
need parents who are sensitive to their style and who neither
neglect their needs to learn to adapt to new situations nor
push them into situations before they are ready. Sensitive
parents offer the Slow-to-Warm-Up Child new opportunities
and gently encourage them, but they do not pressure. They
also avoid holding out a model of a socially gregarious child
before the Slow-to-Warm-Up. Instead, parents learn to value
the carefulness and concern these children show.

Friends of ours have a Slow-to-Warm-Up Child who almost
got them into trouble. For the first eight years or so of his life,
this boy was rather shy and not too sociable. Every time
company came over, the mother tried to force the boy to be
more sociable. She repeatedly told him to "speak up," "look
them in the eyes," and "not act so disinterested." In fact, the
mother would get very angry with her son for behaving in his
quiet, seemingly disinterested way.

Finally the parents realized they were beginning to repeatedly give this boy the message: "We don't like you the
way you are. You should be more outgoing like your sister."
Realizing that this could undercut his self-concept and stir
feelings of resentment, they began to remove the pressure.
They focused on having good times with their son, encouraging him to bring friends home from school and getting him
involved in athletics and other activities. Within a couple of
years the boy was much more outgoing and socially alert. A
combination of their sensitive treatment and his natural
development brought some very significant changes. This boy
will probably never be the clown or cut-up or life of the party,
but he is a very happy, sociable, and delightful lad.

Parents of Difficult Children have to be extremely careful
not to be drawn into a cycle of negativism. If we aren't careful, we can fall into a habit of giving these children attention
when they misbehave. Rather than responding to their good,
cooperative moments, we wait until things go wrong to correct and instruct. Unfortunately this only reinforces the

difficult style. Parents also need to learn to appreciate the
unpredictability and intensity of these children. If we can
learn to set reasonable and consistent limits, keep them constructively occupied, and channel their energy, we can see
these children go far. If, however, we have difficulty relating
to this type of child, he is very likely to develop an image of
himself as the "bad child" or the "problem child." And if he
has problems, they will probably involve getting along with
other people at home or school. The Difficult Child's high
level of spontaneity gets him into trouble.

Thomas and Chess found that no single temperament
characteristic or specific set of traits caused any child to
develop behavioral problems as they grew up. There were
well-adjusted and problem children in each group. When any
of the children had problems, they were caused by a combination of the child's temperament and the family or school environment. Many Difficult Children, for example, got along
great because their parents were not easily upset by their
active, often impulsive style. The parents were able to set
limits carefully and sensitively. Other parents with the same
type of children were unable to control them and suffered
immense guilt and frustration as a result. The key to the
children's adjustment was found to be how well the children
and the parents "fit." That is, were the parents able to tune
into the child's style, appreciate it, and learn to cope in a
positive, accepting, and consistent manner?

A Proverb for Parents

Centuries before psychologists began to study the individual differences of children, the Bible made the very same
point. Sadly many parents, including Christians, have over-
looked this fact and tried to force their children into a prescribed mold or style rather than considering their children's
uniqueness.

A verse in chapter 22 of the Book of Proverbs says this:
"Train a child in the way he should go, and when he is old he

will not turn from it" (v. 6). Many parents have interpreted this verse to mean that if we take our children to Sunday school and church every time the door opens, have family devotions, send them to summer camp, see that they avoid certain sinful activities and stay on the "straight and narrow," they may pass through a period of rebellion and conflict but sometime in their later years will return to the truth! Actually the phrase "in the way he should go" does not refer at all to some prescribed path cut out for every person to follow regardless of his or her individuality.

The word *way* is used in chapter 30 of Proverbs to refer to "the way of an eagle in the sky, the way of a snake on a rock, the way of a ship on the high seas, and the way of a man with a maiden" (vv. 18-19). In every case "the way" refers to a unique, spontaneous direction or style. Theologian Crawford H. Toy put it this way: "In the way he is to go . . . [is] not exactly 'in the path of industry and piety' . . . but 'in accordance with the manner of life to which he is destined.'" In other words, as parents we need to seek out our children's strengths, abilities, and potential, and help them move in the direction in which they point.

We should not take a Slow-to-Warm-Up Child and try to turn him into an outgoing, life-of-the-party, social butterfly. We should not try to transform an Easy Child into a loud, aggressive person. And we should not try to make a Difficult Child become a nice, quiet, and prim and proper person. With age, positive parenting, and broadened experience, all of these children may move a bit in the direction we would like. But our goal should be to find their style and help them channel it in positive directions. If they need some rough edges smoothed out, so be it, but we must always respect their basic God-given temperaments or styles.

Fortunately most marriage partners do not have identical temperaments and at least one partner is able to understand and appreciate the temperament of even the Difficult Child. This is a valuable asset that every parental couple needs to develop. Sometimes we have great difficulty relating to one of our children because his temperament is so totally different from ours that we cannot even comprehend it. A friend of mine, for example, a real "lady," is an outstanding person, extremely well-mannered, sensitive, and socially alert. She knows just how to react in every social situation and wants her children to do the same. Unfortunately one of her children has a very different temperament. As an adolescent the girl couldn't care less about some of her mother's most cherished social values. At times she didn't even *want* to be polite! This practically drove her mother crazy and was the source of much conflict.

At other times we have serious clashes with one of our children simply because we are so much alike. One high-strung, anxious person in the family is plenty. To have a child with the same temperament is just too much! Two easily frustrated and somewhat impulsive people can have serious conflicts.

In a case like this we need to take two steps to avoid serious problems. First, the parent who can most readily understand the child in question needs to take the initiative and do his or her best to value that child and play an active role in the training. Second, the parent in the conflict needs to search out why this child triggers his or her negative responses and learn to appreciate the child's uniqueness and style.

Rather than labeling, condemning, or trying to radically change a child's God-given temperament we need to learn to value it, broaden our own sensitivites, and learn to complement and enjoy the child no matter how different or difficult he seems to be. In other words, we must learn to adapt!

Now, I realize adapting is more easily said than done! We should not expect to accomplish this overnight. We also should not have to give up our own style. If we are born perfectionists, let's accept that. But let's not try to turn our hyperactive, impulsive, aggressive, somewhat bombastic ten-year-old into one! We should set some limits and see that his room has some order and a good measure of cleanliness, but we should not seek to force him into our mold. In fact, we might even come to appreciate his spontaneity and become more flexible ourselves!

Why Are My Children Different?

I am often asked, "Why do two children raised in the same family turn out so differently?" The fact is, no two children (with the possible exception of identical twins) are ever raised in the "same" family. If we have a son and a daughter, our son is being reared in a family with a sister. By contrast, our daughter is being reared with a brother! That is a major difference! And it is not the only one. Unless our children are twins, siblings are either older or younger. And they were born to parents of different ages and differing degrees of experience in parenting! Also, no matter how strongly we may deny it, none of us has identical feelings toward all our children.

There is one more important determinant of our children's personality uniqueness that warrants special attention. That is the children's place in the family constellation.

Being the first child entails both advantages and disadvantages. The first child is often the most cherished. He is mother's first baby, and this evokes some strong feelings from her. At the same time, however, mothers of first children have had no previous practice! They tend to worry excessively over every little detail and take almost incessant care of their "precious little one." This excessive care can communicate anxiety to the infant and make it difficult for him to reach out on his own, try new things, and learn to handle his hurts. Situations that arouse great concern to mothers of first children are often ignored by the time the second or third child comes along, and this more relaxed attitude can really help a child!

When a second child enters the family, the older one encounters more pains and pleasures. As the elder, he probably has more freedom, more responsibility, and more opportunities to do as he pleases. His new brother, however, has obviously replaced him as the baby of the family. The helpless new infant, no matter how wonderful he may be, now has more of mother's time and attention. This can make the older child feel displaced and rejected, and it often stirs feelings of resentment toward the new sibling.

As these children grow, the younger child discovers there are both advantages and disadvantages to being second in line. As the baby he often gets by with murder. He can provoke the older sibling, cry, and see his brother become the object of mother's wrath. He quickly finds all the advantages of being the baby and learns to use them well! At the same time, however, he knows that his brother has more freedom than he does. Brother gets to stay up later and play outside longer, for example. This makes the younger child feel a bit inferior or resentful.

If a third child comes along, everything shifts again. From the position of being the baby, the second son now becomes the "sandwich child." He is sandwiched in between his older brother, who has all the freedoms and privileges of the eldest, and the baby, who has all of the advantages of being the baby! If the parents are not extremely careful, this middle child can become lost in the shuffle. He doesn't have the advantages of either the oldest or the youngest child!

With the arrival of a third child, the eldest is pushed still a

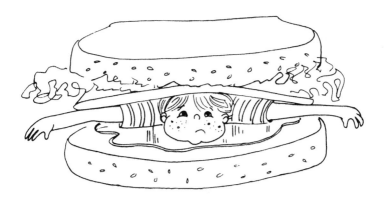

bit further from mother. He may respond with more feelings of isolation or rejection, which he tries to cover by asserting himself physically over one of the younger siblings. If he cannot gain his identity by being close to mother, he might be able to do it by dominating a brother. The eldest may also take full advantage of his position as the most mature. In receiving a larger allowance, staying out longer, staying up later, and in general having more freedom he gains some positive feelings.

The third child, of course, now holds the position of the baby. What he cannot gain through strength, age, and competition, he can gain by being the baby. So, just as the second child may have done, he makes full use of his helplessness to try to manipulate everyone in the family and gain his way as much as possible! Sometimes the first or second child will sense the advantages of being a baby and go through a brief period of regression in which they become more babylike. They regress to baby talk, become more tearful or helpless, and may even lose some of their toilet control.

These feelings and reactions are only a few of the possibilities. Not every child reacts in a typical or expected manner. Yet most children do express some rather predictable reactions suitable to their position in the family structure, and it behooves us to be sensitive to these differences and to the feelings our children are likely to have as a result of this position.

Summary

The rest of this book focuses on some universal human needs and some principles of parenting that apply to every child. Before we move on to these, however, let's summarize the important principles of parenting that grow out of our understanding of children's individual differences.

1. Because of their unique physiological makeup and position in the family, we should expect our children to have different temperaments.
2. Children's temperaments vary widely within a normal range, and there is no one "right" temperament.

3. Since many of our children's reaction tendencies are inborn, we should not blame ourselves for these differences in style.
4. It is always best to flow with our children's basic direction or style rather than to push them into some opposite style.
5. Since all children are different from one another, we must treat them differently if we are to treat them fairly. In other words, we should be flexible in our training and correction so we can meet the needs of all our children.
6. Given sensitive parenting, children with vastly different styles can grow up to be healthy, happy, and productive adults. The difference between styles enriches the world and brings stimulating experiences.
7. Children may have unique struggles or feelings because of their position in the family, and we should be sensitive to these.
8. One of our greatest needs as parents is to learn to value the different styles our children have and learn to flow with them and adapt to them.
9. With good family experiences, time, and other relationships, our children's temperaments tend to mature and the rough edges are rounded off.
10. Despite the great differences between our children, they all share some fundamental emotional and spiritual needs that form the background for important and universal principles of parenting applying to all children.

Part 2

SIX REASONS WHY
CHILDREN MISBEHAVE

Chapter 4

THE ATTENTION-GETTER

Have you ever been preparing a meal for company or doing some other task at home when your daughter walked in and asked, "Will you play with me?" If you are like most of us, the chances are you replied, "I'm sorry, sweetheart, but I'm busy right now." Somewhat disappointed the girl turns away and busies herself for the next few minutes. But before long she is back again. "Mommy (or daddy)," she asks with a bit more urgency, "will you play with me now?" "Maybe later honey," you reply, "I have to get things ready for dinner now and I just don't have the time." Once again your child trudges off, but this time she is obviously unhappy. She feels left out and unimportant. She feels like a second-class person compared with the company you have on your mind.

You return to your work, but after a while you realize it has been extremely quiet a little too long. You decide to investigate and, sure enough, as you start down the hall, you detect the aroma of your most expensive perfume, or you see some beautiful artistic creation on the wall, or you find the end of the roll of toilet paper yards from its original source! As you track it down, you are amazed at how many feet of paper there

are in one small roll! Or if you have more than one child, this scenario takes a different tack. Instead of thirty minutes of "dangerous silence," your rebuffed daughter goes to the other end of the house and starts hassling her brother. Before long, they are on the verge of war!

In both instances, your daughter is giving you a message. She is saying "Mother (or dad), if you won't pay any attention to me when I am being good, then I will get into trouble to gain your attention." And notice what you did. You played right into her game. When things become dangerously silent, or when your daughter provoked a conflict with her brother, you gave her just the attention she was seeking through her actions. You rewarded or reinforced her attention-getting misbehavior!

Most of our children's misbehaviors and problems operate on this principle. When their basic physical and emotional needs are not met, they turn to substitutes or counterfeits. Children who are feeling lonely, rejected, isolated, or left out, for example, frequently turn to attention-getting misbehavior. They know that if they cause enough commotion, their parents will come running and give them the attention they desire! What parent can ignore a budding Rembrandt who has chosen the living room wall as his canvas? What parent can ignore two screaming children engaged in hand-to-hand combat? And what parent can ignore a teen-ager who is on drugs, breaking curfew, or failing Sophomore English?

God created every person with a set of basic emotional, physical, and social needs and assigned parents the major responsibility for meeting these needs. Every child, through adolescence for example, needs to feel loved and know that he belongs. Every child needs to know that he is a significant, important person. And every child needs to feel adequate and competent. When these needs are not effectively met, children begin to feel lonely, depressed, anxious, or insecure. And since no one enjoys these negative emotions, they quickly learn a number of techniques for temporarily warding off these painful feelings and finding substitutes for what is lacking.

The steps leading up to our children's problems usually go this way:

1. Our child has a need or a wish;
2. This need or wish is not fulfilled;
3. Our child begins to feel discouraged, lonely, unappreciated, insignificant, anxious, or inferior;
4. To avoid these negative feelings he acts in ways that bring substitute or counterfeit gratification; these actions are usually undesirable and hurtful both to the child and to the family;
5. We react to our children's misdirected ways of trying to satisfy their needs in ways that perpetuate the problem.

God-Given Need:	When Need Is Not Met:	Child Turns to Substitute of:
Love	Loneliness and Isolation	Attention

Let me pose a frank question: When do you give your children your most complete attention? When do you lay everything else aside and focus totally and completely on your sons and daughters? Is it when they are well-mannered, cooperative, and constructively occupying themselves? Or is it when they have interrupted your activities with fussing, fighting, or crying?

Many of us will have to admit that we give our children our clearest, best, and fullest attention when they misbehave. As long as they are happily busying themselves in front of the television, in their own rooms, or with a friend, we go about our work and pay them little mind. But as soon as they get in trouble, we come running. We drop whatever we are doing, go to them, look them in the eye, and give them our complete and undivided attention. At that moment they are the only focus of our attention. But consider what we have done: we have unthinkingly rewarded their misbehavior by giving them exactly what they wanted—our complete attention!

In part 2 we will examine how this vicious cycle works.

Each chapter will examine one or two of our children's God-given needs and show how our failure to help our children satisfy these needs causes many of the frustrating conflicts and hassles we encounter daily as parents. Then we will explore what we can do to meet our children's needs more effectively so they will be less inclined to turn to substitutes. Once we recognize how this works, we will be able to prevent or reduce a large number of family conflicts and be well on our way to a more rewarding and peaceful family existence.

Parents Are People Too!

Adults are not much different from children. In fact, one of the best ways of understanding our children's needs and wishes is to put ourselves in their place. Let's say you are a wife who occasionally gets a little "down" or "blue." You sometimes feel a bit unloved and try a variety of things to gain the attention and reassurance you want. Perhaps you feel like a television widow—it is football season, and your husband spends every weekend plus Monday evening in front of the TV set. You feel like the woman who said, "The only way my husband would know I had died is if they announced it on 'Wide World of Sports'!"

Since your husband comes home tired from work on the evenings when he isn't watching television, the two of you spend practically no quality time together. After several months (or years) of this you are getting down. You need your husband's encouragement and support. You want to know he loves you. So you fix him a special meal—his very favorite— but he gulps it down as usual. You sit beside him on the couch and ask, "Honey, do you love me?" He grunts some semi-intelligible reply but remains glued to the TV or the newspaper. You try several other tactics, but nothing seems to work. Finally, in desperation you walk over and stand between him and the television set. Or, if you are a little bolder or a bit more desperate, you click it off! You know before you do it how your husband will respond: he will become angry and probably yell at you to turn it on! But even though you knew your actions would upset him, you did it anyway! Why? Because you wanted some attention. And negative attention is better than no attention at all! You would rather have him angry at you than be ignored. You might even throw out a sarcastic remark like "My, it's nice to see you are alive and breathing!"

Our children operate on exactly the same principle. Many times they look for trouble simply to force us to give them more attention. Even before they start they have a good idea we will be upset, but they go full steam ahead. Moreover, it is precisely because they know we will be upset that they persist!

Let's take a look at our children's most important emotional need—the need for love—and see how we can help them meet this need and avoid turning to substitute, attention-getting misbehaviors.

Love Is Not Enough

Several years ago I returned home from a series of meetings on the East Coast. My plane arrived in Los Angeles around 8:30 in the evening, and by the time I got my baggage to the car and drove home, it was nearly ten o'clock. I was still on Baltimore time, however, and that made it feel more like 2:00 A.M. I was very tired and really looking forward to getting home and falling into bed.

I parked the car in the driveway, took out my briefcase and suitcase, and walked toward the house. Just as I reached for the doorknob I heard an awful crash and one of the children crying. I opened the door, and there were Dickie and Debbie, both crying, on the floor with an overturned coffee table between them. I had had a hard day and didn't need this kind of a welcome!

My first impulse was to yell, "What's the matter with you anyway? I just got home and you are already fighting!" I felt like telling them to "shut up, go to your rooms, and leave me alone!" It was past their bedtime anyway, and I was in no mood for this kind of hassle. Fortunately I got my wits about me and thought, "What would you tell someone else to do in this kind of a mess?"

Then I realized what was going on. I had been away for a couple of days. Before that I had been extra busy at work. For nearly a week I really hadn't had any quality time with the children. They both missed me and had been racing to the door to see which one could greet me first! They were running, in other words, to get my love! But when I first saw and heard them in that pile, I certainly didn't recognize their search for love! Only when I stepped back for a moment and asked myself what was happening could I understand the source of my disturbing welcome.

As soon as I realized what was happening, I sat down on the couch and said, "Dickie, come here." With a serious look on his face Dickie came over and sat down on my lap. I said, "Son, how would you like me to take you to school tomorrow morning? We could leave a few minutes early and go to McDonald's for breakfast on the way." Immediately Dickie brightened up. "Oh boy!" he exclaimed as he jumped up and headed on his way.

Then I called for Debbie. "Climb up here on my lap, honey," I said. And she did. How about on Friday morning you and I go out for breakfast? Would you like to go to McDonald's, or would you rather go to Sambo's?" "Sambo's," Debbie immediately replied, since Dickie had chosen to go to McDonald's! And she was on her way!

Then I looked across the room and saw my wife with a threatening look in her eyes. "Honey," I said, "come sit on my lap!" And then I asked her if she would like to go out to dinner the next evening!

After a few more minutes of family time we put the children to bed and had our peace and quiet. The whole thing didn't take five minutes, and the atmosphere in our house went from complete chaos to real tranquility. All it took was the time to think, "Why are my children misbehaving?" And as soon as that was realized, I could do a little something that took care of their needs.

I share this little incident to make a very important point: *love is not enough.* One of the most subtle traps well-meaning parents can fall into is the assumption that all our children need is love. We read that "love covers a multitude of sins" and we just assume that if we love our children, everything will eventually turn out fine. But psychologists' offices are filled with people whose parents loved them. For some reason the parents' love didn't get through. There was a gap between the parents' love for their children and their ability to communicate it. It is not enough to love our children. We must not be satisfied until we learn to communicate our love in ways they can understand and accept.

I suppose all parents love their children. Even parents with serious problems and strong resentments harbor at least some positive emotions for their children. And because most of us love our children deeply, we assume they know how much we love them. In fact, we often assume it is our children's responsibility to know how much we love them. We brought them into the world and provided all their physical needs. We cook and clean and work to support them. And we love them. So we naturally assume they know we love them. Our love is so obvious to us that, as one father put it, "only a fool could miss it!" But unfortunately this is not the case. There is frequently a big gap between our love for our children and our ability to express it in ways that our children can understand. It is one thing to love our children; it is quite another for them to feel our love daily.

Our children need a deep awareness of their belonging. Children need to feel that they are an integral part of our families. They need to be listened to. They need to have their wishes and feelings taken into consideration. They need our time. And most of all, they need to see from our actions that they are our top priority.

When Children Feel Unloved

When I speak of children not feeling loved, I do not necessarily mean they are walking around feeling sorry for themselves, reflecting on how lonely and unloved they are, and contemplating some drastic action like suicide! The feeling of being unloved can show itself in a sense of loneliness, in the feeling of being disliked, in the feeling that one is a bother to someone else, or in simply feeling left out. And it can show itself in the feeling of not being understood. Barb, a seventeen-year-old high school senior, put it this way: "My most difficult struggle is not feeling understood. I have never had any heart-to-heart talks with my mother, and I can't discuss anything with my parents open-mindedly."

Children who lack a deep sense of love and acceptance express this in a number of ways. Some simply give in to these feelings and become depressed. Some become constantly noisy and restless, wondering what to do. Some become smart alecks or showoffs. Some become hostile and belligerent. And some seek from other sources the love they don't feel they are getting at home.

Teen-age girls who become excessively boy-crazy and adolescents who marry early or engage in premarital sex are frequently looking for a substitute for the love they do not experience at home. One parent, reflecting on her teen-age years, told me, "My mother was a single parent and had little time to notice me or to listen. Consequently I would do anything to be accepted, especially by my peers. It turned out that the way I could be most accepted was by giving up my virginity and becoming promiscuous. For years I was accepted mainly because I was sexy. I devoured any kind of attention, so I continued my loose sexual activity."

Another parent wrote me this note about her adolescent search for love:

> The most difficult struggle I had as a teen-ager was not being able to communicate with my father. I wanted to be

close and comfortable with him, but he was awkward about
showing his love for me.

I became boy-crazy at fourteen and realized a loved feeling
from a man for my first time. From then on, I lived from one
date to the next. I accepted a substitute for love—belonging to
a steady—instead of learning to love.

I have carried this vacuum into my marriage. I deeply want
to be loved, but I have trouble accepting it when it's there. I
keep busy and occupied to keep from getting too close because
I am afraid I will be hurt again. Recently I have realized I need
to learn to love and be loved, but I don't know how to begin.

Both these women saw the deep hurt and conflicts caused by
their failure to experience a deep sense of love and belonging
during crucial adolescent years. Others who experience similar feelings of loneliness or rejection may respond in a different way. Boys in particular may steel themselves against inti-
macy, put on a front, and act as though they really don't need
love! Unfortunately this cuts them off from deep, enriching
relationships and can leave them feeling sterile and empty
inside. It can also make for great difficulty in marriage, especially if the partner has a strong need for love and reassurance.

Parents' Priorities

Our children's feelings of loneliness and isolation usually
come from one of two sources. The first is the amount of time
we spend with them; the second is the quality. "Quality"
basically boils down to our ability to listen sympathetically to
our children, to value their ideas and feelings, and to enjoy
our times together. A simple but helpful formula is *Understanding + Enjoyment = Feelings of Love.* Since understanding our children is really the subject of this entire book,
we will only mention it in passing here. We will give more
attention to the amount of time we spend with our children.

Even the most loving of us can fall into a busy routine that
unknowingly robs our family of times of real togetherness and
love. Especially as our children grow older and enter their
teens, we can start to go in a thousand different directions.

We are chauffeuring one child to band, another to gym, and a third to an athletic event or a church activity. We have a bundle of responsibilities at work or at home, and the only time all our paths cross at once is at mealtimes or briefly on the way to church.

There is nothing inherently wrong with these activities. But somehow they have gotten out of hand and are robbing us of the single most important thing a family can provide: a deep sense of belonging and the feeling of being loved and understood. Love that is hidden in our hearts or expressed largely through what we do *for* others is not sufficient. If our children are genuinely going to grasp our love, we must find ways of really being *with* them. We must have some quiet times together. We must take time to listen to their thoughts, their feelings, and their experiences. Moments of quiet, complete attention do more to communicate our love than almost any other single thing. They also do more to prevent family problems and conflicts than anything I know!

If you find your family slipping into a "busy cycle," it may be helpful to sit down and make a careful evaluation of your priorities. Write out and discuss the most important things in life to you. List them in order of priority: our mates, our children, and our relationship with God are usually high on our priority lists. Then make a chart showing the way you actually spend your time. List the amount of time you spend sleeping, working, watching television, in social activities, at church, and in the car and anywhere else that is a familiar scene in your life. Then list the amount of time you spend alone with your sons and daughters on an average day. List only the times you are really together—talking, playing, or in some way sharing. Do not count time sitting in the same room reading or watching television as "Together Time"! Now compare your list of priorities with the way you actually spend your time.

If you are like most parents, you will find that the things (and people) at the top of your list of priorities are near the bottom of the chart that reflects the way you spend your time! One of the most life-changing actions your family can take is to sit down with the list and rearrange the schedule so that you can spend more time on what you really value and less on other things.

There are naturally some practical limitations to rearranging our schedules. The family breadwinner cannot quit his job and stay home all day with the children. We need regular times of worship and fellowship with others. And there are a number of tasks like cooking, cleaning, and yard work that must be done. But most of us waste time in unessential activities. We lose time through poor planning and preparation. And we spend a lot of time in activities that, while not wrong in themselves, force us to minimize or neglect more important activities.

Several years ago my wife and I sat down to think through our relationships with our children. We loved them very much and wanted the best for them. But Kathy and I also tend to be very active, busy people. We didn't want to wake up twenty years later and say, "What happened? We loved our children and did the best we could. What went wrong?"

To keep this from happening, we sat down and talked through the whole matter of our lifestyle. I would come home tired and not feel like playing with the children. Kathy was often so busy entertaining or leading study groups that she found herself unable to give the children as much of her time as they needed. We evaluated our priorities and came up with a couple of solutions. Kathy decided to cancel a seminar she was about to teach on parenting! She saw that it would be impossible to give our children the time they needed at the same time she was helping other mothers relate to their children! I decided to find some way to relax and unwind at the end of a day and still do some fun things with the children.

About that time some friends told us about Lego blocks. These are a marvelous toy because they are small and indestructible and functional! You can build anything with Lego blocks. If you had enough, you might even be able to build a house and live in it!

Dickie and I went downtown and bought our first batch of Lego blocks and came home and started building. At first we built a basic log cabin kind of house—four walls, a roof, and a door. But as our architectural skills improved, we became more daring. We built larger houses. We built a fire station. And we built a battery-powered train that would actually run on a small track! At first I felt a little awkward getting on the floor and playing blocks with my children. "After all," I thought, "I am a Ph.D. psychologist. I work in a think-factory. Isn't this a little beneath my dignity?" But soon I realized I was enjoying playing with the blocks. In fact, I found I could relax and unwind better at the end of a hard day's work playing blocks with my children than I could watching the six o'clock news or reading the newspaper!

Beginning with that experience, I have learned to really enjoy my children. I must admit that it did not come easily. I grew up on a farm in Arizona where there was not much playtime. My father would get up early to feed the cattle or do other chores before breakfast. Then he would put in ten or twelve more hours of work. After school and in the summers my brother and I were expected to do our share. Although we had plenty of opportunities to play alone or with each other, my brother and I did not share a lot of opportunities to just relax and play with our father. He was tired after a full day's work and didn't feel like throwing around a football, working on a jigsaw puzzle, or playing the latest fad game.

When I became a parent, I began to follow this same style. As I began seeing my children's need for time with me, I had to work at making time. Only gradually did I learn to cut out extraneous activities or drop some things that I was doing to spend more time with the children. But as I did, I learned some very important lessons. To begin with, I found out that I was a workaholic: one thing I needed most was to learn to relax and enjoy life. I found out that playing with my children enriched my life as well as theirs. And I found that my marriage was strengthened by family fun. Right now Dickie and Debbie both play on the local soccer team. I help coach the team (even though I knew nothing about soccer when I started), so I can be involved in their activities. We also play indoor games together and talk a lot and enjoy each other's company.

The mutual enjoyment our family shares together, however, is only one of the blessings of learning to enjoy each other. When children are enjoying themselves and feeling loved and accepted, they do not have to turn to misbehavior for attention. When we have the real thing, we don't need to look for the substitute! I am firmly convinced that a very significant portion of our children's misbehavior could be eradicated if we would only learn to spend more and better time with our children and really communicate our love. Happy children with a true sense of belonging are much less likely to get into difficulty than children whose parents are too busy to spend quality time with them regularly.

The Television Trap

When our daughter Debbie was about two years old, our television set went on the blink. This was fairly early in our marriage, and we decided not to repair it for a while. In just a couple of weeks we noticed a real change in our family atmosphere. Kathy and I were communicating more. We were spending more time with the children. And in general we were experiencing "togetherness." We decided we would forget the television for the time being and continue to enjoy other activities together. A year or so later we decided we had matured enough to manage our TV rather than letting it manage us, so we invested in a small portable set. Unfortunately I am the kind of person who will walk up and turn on the set just to see whether anything good is on. And I always like to watch the ten o'clock news and the Monday evening football game. Dickie and Debbie, needless to say, also started to spend a great deal of time watching the TV. Soon we noticed much of our time was starting to revolve around the television. We had fewer fun times together and were becoming passive rather than active participants in family living. Finally we made a difficult decision. We called Goodwill Industries and asked them to take the set off our hands!

We have been without a television set for nearly ten years now, and I am happy to report that its absence has been a blessing to our family. Our children are avid readers and do well in school in part because we have no television. They are active rather than passive learners because they have had to search things out on their own in the library and in the books they read. And we have much more time together as a family. In fact, several years ago we were returning from vacation and Dickie (then eight) was reading a newspaper. All of a sudden he exclaimed, "Hey, dad, look at this!" He read to me a brief article that said ninety-nine out of every one hundred homes in the United States have at least one television. After reading the item, he said with a bit of pride, "Hey, dad, we're in the one percent!" He took pride in knowing we were not like everyone else. On a couple of occasions, in fact, I have overheard our children explaining to their friends that we don't have television because "we like to do fun things together as a family!"

Please don't misunderstand me. We watch TV occasionally at a friend's home, and we periodically visit grandmother in order to see a certain program. It seems to me, however, that there is a great deal of bad programming on television that can't help but subtly undermine our children's values; and even good programs can become a habit that reaches almost to the point of addiction. A group of researchers in Detroit offered 120 families $500 to do without television for one month's time, and ninety-three of the families refused the offer! They didn't believe it was worth $500 to give up television for one month! I find that hard to believe. It seems to me they could at least have taken the $500, abstained for thirty

days, and then used the money to purchase a new color set! But apparently the addiction was too strong. And the twenty-seven families who accepted the offer had some very unusual experiences. Nearly all of them initially reported periods of boredom, nervousness, and depression. They were so unaccustomed to entertaining themselves that at first they didn't know what to do.

Some friends of ours have come up with a less drastic solution to the TV problem than total abstinence. They purchase *TV Guide* every Saturday, sit down as a family, and decide what programs they will watch during the next week. They impose a limit of about an hour each day, and the programs must be selected ahead of time. This allows them to choose good programs and averts the possibility of just clicking on the tube when they "don't know what else to do."

The power of television was demonstrated in a study reported in *Psychology Today* a few years ago.[1] The researchers found that nearly half of the twelve-year-olds they surveyed watch television for an average of six or more hours each day! Dividing TV watchers into light watchers (two hours or less daily) and heavy watchers (four or more hours daily), the researchers discovered that heavy watchers were more likely to view the real world as dangerous and violent than light watchers. The researchers concluded that the heavy diet of television violence instilled fear in heavy viewers and caused them to be significantly more distrustful of other people and to overestimate their chances of being the victim of violence.

My prime concern here, however, is not to stress the possible negative influences of television. There are many good programs for both children and adults. When viewed selectively, television can be a positive influence and an effective educational instrument. My purpose is to suggest that television is one of the forces in our culture that can subtly split the family apart and keep us from taking time to think through some truly uplifting and constructive activities we could enjoy together. I realize that watching television is often the easiest thing to do: we can simply fall into a chair and turn on the tube. That's much easier than getting dressed and going out. It's easier than going outside and playing catch or even taking a table game off the shelf and having a family game night. But watching television tends to be an isolating rather than a uni-

---

[1]"The Scary World of TV's Heavy Viewer" in *Psychology Today* (April 1976).

fying experience. Active participation in a family activity is much more enriching and ultimately rewarding than repeated watching of television dramas.

The Sky's the Limit

In this chapter I have tried to communicate the great importance of learning to communicate our love to our children in ways that they can understand and acknowledge. The Bible tells us that "children are a gift of the Lord" (Ps. 127:3); we are "to delight in them" (Prov. 3:12). When we take stock of our priorities and learn to really enjoy our children, we do ourselves and them a big favor. Our children feel important and loved. They develop a positive outlook on life. And they will not have to turn to various kinds of misbehavior in a frustrated search for attention. At the same time we profit by finding what joy our children can bring to us. We can learn to relax and enjoy life more. And we can learn to put our priorities more on rewarding relationships with people than we do on our work or on possessions.

My purpose in this book is not to suggest specific activities for us to engage in with our children. Every family is different. Some are very outdoor-oriented; others are more the indoor type. But the number of interesting activities is almost unlimited. The main thing is that we learn to enjoy each other. We are the most important gift we can give our children, and they are God's most important gift to us.

Chapter 5

WHO'S IN CHARGE?

If you have a young child—up to seven years of age perhaps —you are probably two or three times his size. He may weigh forty or fifty pounds, but you probably weigh between one and two hundred. You are also a great deal taller than your child. To see things from your child's perspective, let's imagine that two people are assigned to you who are three times your size. They are each eighteen feet tall and weigh five hundred pounds! These giants follow you everywhere you go. They repeatedly tell you "Hurry up," "Slow down," "Speak up," and "Quiet down." One of these giants cooks your food. The other one makes you eat it. You call one of them mother and the other father! Everywhere you go, these giants are watching over you. They tell you what you can and cannot do.

This sort of arrangement most likely would not instill in you a great amount of self-confidence! Although you would appreciate your giants providing and protecting you, you would also feel a bit inferior. You wouldn't have a lot of confidence.

But let's back up a little further. Take the newborn infant lying in the crib. He doesn't even know that he exists! He realizes something has happened. The lights are bright and

"I paint what I see."

something is different, but at this stage of his development the infant literally does not know that he exists as a separate person. His central nervous system has not developed to the point where he can even tell the difference between himself and his mother.

Gradually this situation changes. The infant begins to recognize certain objects. He finds that some of these go with him everywhere he goes—for example, his hands, feet, and toes. He finds that others are not always present—chairs, blankets, and toys. He also finds that certain of these things—hands, feet and toes—have a special kind of feeling. They are different from "those other things." Slowly the infant begins to put this all together. He realizes that the feet, hands, and toes all belong to him. Then he comes to realize that he is a separate person—even different from his mother! This happens gradually during the first twelve months of life.

At about a year of age, the average child takes his first few steps and utters his first real words. Soon his favorite words after "dada" and "mama" are "my," "me," and "mine!" Not only does he know he is a separate person, but he is also beginning to gather his possessions to prove just who he is and what is his! By the time the child turns two, he is really getting to like the idea of being an independent person. When we say no, he says yes. When we say "black," he says "white." Whatever we say to the two-year-old, he is likely to take the opposite approach. This is why some child development experts have labeled this period "the Terrible Twos." Two years ago this young person didn't even exist. One year ago he was just learning to move around a bit and communicate with his first few words. He lives in a world of giants, and he doesn't feel very strong, intelligent, or confident. One of the few ways open to him for demonstrating his own strength is to do the opposite of what others say.

At about this point many parents decide to toilet-train their youngsters. This can be a big mistake! We tell our child, "Mommy (or daddy) wants you to do it in here when we tell you." The child thinks to himself, "I will do it in my pants anytime I please." There are, we discover, some things that even a giant cannot force people to do, and this is one of them! So we set the child on the potty, and he just sits there. We let him stay for lengthy periods and nothing happens. Finally we give up, assuming that he doesn't really need to go. And five minutes later, what happens? Yes, he has gone in his pants again!

Now, what is the problem here? Does our child have a physical problem? Perhaps. Is he not bright enough to understand? Perhaps. Or is he not physically ready to be trained? Possibly. But time after time I have found that there is no physical or intellectual problem. The child is simply taking this opportunity to exert his power and to prove to us and to himself that he has a mind of his own! He is in a gigantic power struggle.

This glimpse at our child's first two years of life helps explain one of the main dilemmas every person faces as a child. How can he develop a healthy sense of confidence in his own abilities since he is so small and relatively helpless?

We all know a few people who always have to have their way. In a committee meeting the decisions must agree with their opinions. In a discussion they must always have the last word. If the family is going out for dinner, everyone has to go where they want to go and when they want to. In a thousand ways these people attempt to control everyone around them and exert their power or authority. When we first meet these people, we often see them as confident and aggressive. We respect their good ideas and their ability to assume leadership and express their feelings and commitments. But as we get to know them better we begin to notice an underlying pattern. It seems as if they *always* have to have their way. They are not simply aggressive: they are dogmatic and demanding. They are seldom able to do things someone else's way.

If we could see beneath the surface of these people's personalities we would find quite a different picture from the external, confident one we are so used to seeing. In fact, under that confident exterior we would probably find a very frightened, inferior-feeling person. What seems at first glance to be confidence is actually a counterfeit. It is an external trapping designed to hide the absence of the very attributes the person tries so hard to show.

Truly confident people do not have to argue, control, or pressure others in order to gain their way. People with a deep inner sense of confidence can express their opinions but also be flexible. They can go with the majority and listen to and respect the opinions of others. Because they are inwardly confident, they don't have to attempt to gain power or control.

Our children operate on exactly the same dynamic. If they feel confident, they can speak up, express their desires, and freely interact with others. But if they lack confidence, they will either withdraw and assume a helpless, dependent kind of lifestyle or repeatedly attempt to make up for their underlying lack of confidence by gaining power or controlling others. This search for power is one of the most important dynamics operating in every home, and it helps to explain many family conflicts. To understand more fully how it operates, let's take a look at the three options facing our children for gaining a sense of confidence.

Fight Power With Power

The first option is that children can become stubborn, learn to fight, and continually look for ways of circumventing their parents' authority and proving their own strength. This is the solution many children choose. They become negativistic. They become stubborn. They question every decision. And they find a hundred ways to frustrate us to prove that they are people too. As they grow older they refuse to take out the trash, clear the table, clean their rooms, or do any of their chores without a dozen naggings. As teen-agers they become sassy, sullen, negativistic, or rebellious. In all this they are attempting to say, "You can't tell me what to do. I am a person all by myself!"

Sometimes the rebellion is extremely subtle. Since the child knows he is physically inferior to his parents, he doesn't dare stand up to them directly. If he frontally challenged their authority and refused to cooperate, they might use their superior power to force him into conformity. To avoid this ominous occurrence, the child learns to passively resist our

God-Given Need:	When Need Is Not Met:	Child Turns to Substitute of:
Confidence	Weakness, Anxiety, Inferiority	Power

admonitions. The child who is always late, for example, is frequently expressing a passive form of control. No matter how much we pressure and exhort, he is always late. Beneath his pleasant exterior, he is stubbornly saying, "You will not pressure me to do what you want when you want! I will be my own person. I will do this when I am ready!"

Many adults are the same way. We are perpetually late. If it is a morning activity, we never arrive quite on time. Vowing to overcome our habit, we wake up a few minutes early (or our spouse attempts to get us moving); but even though we start earlier we are still a little late. Then we get up a half-hour early—but still we don't quite make it. The fact is that we want to be late! Unconsciously we do not want to be on time! We are inwardly saying, "I don't care how badly you want to be there on time, you are not going to pressure me. I will leave when I am good and ready!" We are being passively rebellious against either our mate or our internal pressures. If we look into the background of a person like this, we nearly always find a nagging or pressuring parent who tried to motivate the child through repeated "suggestions," pressuring, or nagging. The child's only apparent recourse was passive rebellion.

If You Can't Lick 'Em, Join 'Em

A second way young children can attempt to cope with their feelings of inferiority and lack of confidence is to adopt a weak and helpless style of life. Fearing reprimand and punishment for violating their parents' will, these children "identify with the aggressor." Their motto is, "If you can't lick 'em, join 'em!" But not only do they join the "enemy"; they actually find some very sneaky ways to turn these parent-giants into servants: they *always* ask them what to do. They won't venture out without a giant's presence. They cry a lot—and often succeed in getting their way. Because the children feel inferior, the giants spend extra time with them. And the giants do things for them that they wouldn't do for more confident children.

Such a child covers his lack of confidence and gains power in two ways. By endearing himself cooperatively to his parents he is assured of their protection and favor: what he lacks, they will provide. And by being weak and helpless he motivates them to give him even more: his weakness becomes a way of manipulating others in desired directions.

A Cooperative Solution

Both options that we have discussed for overcoming a person's sense of weakness and inadequacy leave much to be desired. If allowed to go unchecked, they may become lifelong patterns that continue essentially unchanged into one's adulthood. At that time they will show up in marriage, at work, and in all interpersonal relationships. The third option is one that requires the parents' help. Since we parents are obviously the ones with power in the young child's world, we hold the key to the development of our children's sense of confidence. We can unknowingly drive our children toward either a fearful-dependent controlling style of coping or an externally rebellious or controlling style. The key to this is our handling of our own power and our sensitivity to our children's needs for confidence.

Every parent must struggle with the problem of authority, confidence, and power. Unfortunately we often go to one extreme or the other. We become so bent on teaching our children obedience and respect for authority that we undercut their self-esteem and need for confidence. Or, in trying to encourage our children to develop positive attitudes toward themselves, we become permissive and allow them to grow up without much-needed discipline. The solution to this problem lies in our own attitudes toward confidence, power, and respect.

The Bible tells us that God has placed parents in a position of authority over children. We are instructed to train (Prov. 22:6), instruct (Prov. 4:1), and discipline our children (Prov. 23:13). There are two ways, however, of teaching respect. The first is to try to prove to our children that we are the ones in control. Since we are bigger and since God has placed us in a position of authority, we are going to be sure our children know it. When they confront us rebelliously, we are going to take the opportunity to show them who is boss. We think that in doing this we are fulfilling our God-given responsibility to teach children to respect authority. But this is totally untrue.

It is absolutely impossible to *prove* to our children who is boss. The moment we attempt to do so we have fallen into a trap. We have assumed that parental authority is something to be won so our emphasis is placed on winning. But every fight has to have a winner and a loser. If we win through pure power, our children end up losing. Their self-esteem is undermined. Their healthy self-assertiveness is squelched—at least temporarily—and they develop feelings of resentment toward us and all authorities.

God did not design a system where our children's self-esteem and confidence have to be attacked in order to learn respect for authority. His plan is to make both parents and children feel good about themselves and each other. This is not accomplished by fighting for authority. *Our job is to win our children over, not win over our children.*

In God's system, parents operate on delegated authority. We *have* authority because God gives it to us. Authority is not something we fight for; it is something we already possess. Our role as parents, therefore, is to lovingly exercise our authority rather than to fight for it. The minute we start fighting for control, our children know who is really in control. *They* are! *They* have made us lose our temper, and *they* have caused us to get upset. *We* are the ones who are ranting and raving, and *we* are the ones who are fighting or yelling or showing that we are not in control of ourselves. Even when we force children to comply with our demands, they cannot respect us. They may be afraid of our power and our temper, but that is not respect: it is fear. Respect is earned by acting respectably, and parental fits of yelling, nagging, and physical abuse are not respectable. They are sure signs that we have panicked. We are threatened and we feel unable to cope with our rebellious children unless we throw a tantrum of our own!

When we fight power with power, our children are the losers. Even though we may gain external conformity, we are prompting very undesirable attitudes inside. As one little boy defiantly said when his mother made him sit in the corner, "Inside I'm still standing up!"

A better way of handling our children's confrontations is to work calmly from our own inner sense of confidence. Now, I realize this is easier said than done. We may not have much confidence in our ability to correct our children. We may be easily upset and anxious. And we may fear that our children can run all over us. Having these feelings, the only thing we know to do is to fight back—to fight power with power—or to throw up our hands and threaten them with that timeworn line "Just wait 'till dad comes home!" But this doesn't have to

be. We *can* learn to handle even difficult situations. We may
not learn it overnight, but we can learn. The keys are to
understand ourselves, our children, and a few effective principles of discipline.

Avoiding the Power Struggle

When I asked a group of adults to write a few paragraphs on
the most difficult thing about being a parent, Fran, the
mother of two-year-old Reuben, wrote, "I just can't handle it
when he deliberately disobeys. Since the day he turned two,
Reuben hardly ever obeys a command. First I ask him; then I
plead; then I threaten; and then I yell. He just goes about his
business or yells 'No!' I have tried spanking, and it works for a
while, but before long he's acting up again." Joanie, the mother
of another two-year-old, echoed Fran's dilemma when she
wrote, "When Michael gets in one of his stubborn moods, I
get so angry I have my own childish outburst. Sometimes I
feel like I ought to be wearing diapers too!"

Fran and Joanie had a common problem—especially for parents of two-year-olds. They were being drawn into a power
struggle because they didn't know how to handle their children's negativism.

Many hassles with our children boil down to this "power
struggle."[1] The power struggle is essentially a fight for control
between a parent and a child. We ask a child to do something,
and he refuses; we ask him to stop doing something, and he
continues. In one way or another he is bound and determined
to "show us who is boss."

These struggles have two causes. One is the child's inferior
position and his natural feeling of smallness and inadequacy.
Because he is weak in relation to his parents, he naturally

---

[1]Rudolf Dreikurs and Vicki Soltz popularized the concept of the power struggle in
their helpful book *Children: The Challenge* (New York: Hawthorn, 1964). Unfortunately they hold a humanistic view of human nature that sees children as essentially
good (or at least neutral) and consequently propound a democratic form of family
government rather than a loving, sensitive authority.

wants to find ways of improving his confidence and showing that he can accomplish things. This is a natural and God-given wish. We all need to find ourselves as persons and learn to exercise our developing minds and bodies by doing things on our own.

Along with this healthy desire, however, is a less noble one. Since the time of Adam and Eve, all human beings have had a tendency to want things their own way. We all prefer to do what *we* want to do. If we had our way we would not have *anybody* telling us what to do. In other words, we would like the complete power to control our own lives. We would like to be our own gods!

This innate tendency to want to run our own lives merges with the child's healthy desire for confidence to set the struggle for power in motion. Any exertion of authority by a parent is potentially a challenge to a child to show that he has a mind of his own. If we want to avoid repeated hassles over a thousand issues, we must learn to recognize when our children are drawing us into a power struggle and remove ourselves before the battle starts. Sometimes, of course, this is not easy to do. We may not even be aware that our children have drawn us into battle. It may be hours later before we wake up to what has happened. But as we become sensitive to our children's drive for power and control, we can avoid being pulled into these conflicts.

Probably the best way to sense an impending power struggle is to monitor our own feelings. The moment we become angry with a child and want to set him straight, force him to do what we want, or show him who is boss, it is very likely that we are headed for a power struggle. Our child's fight for power, in other words, has stirred our own need to prove we are in control.

Several years ago I called Dickie in from play to go to his grandmother's house for dinner. "I'm not going," Dickie announced in response to my call.

My first impulse was to say, "Oh yes, you are! I told you to come in and get ready and you had better get in here!" He had challenged my authority, and I was prepared to show him who was boss! I quickly caught myself, however, and realized what was going on. Dickie was in the middle of some activity; he was enjoying himself and didn't want to be disturbed. The last thing on his mind was going to grandmother's for supper. I also realized that he was about to draw me into a power struggle. He had issued a challenge, and I was ready to do battle! But knowing these conflicts never have a happy ending, I backed off.

With strong feeling, I said, "You really don't want to go to grandmother's, do you?"

"No!" he said firmly, but with less anger. "I'm not going!"

"Are we interrupting your game?" I inquired.

"Yes," he said, "and I want to finish."

"I understand that Dickie," I replied. "Sometimes I have to do something I don't want, and I get angry too! I know it's hard to stop your game, but we told grandmother we would be over at six and we have to leave now."

Still not happy, but a bit more understanding, he came into the house and prepared to leave.

I could have forced Dickie to "get in here" at the very first. But that would have stirred his anger and resentment, and it would not have been considerate of his feelings. None of us likes to be interrupted, so his reaction to my call was a natural one. By letting him know that I understood his feelings, I showed him I respected him—I wasn't just trying to boss him. We had a commitment that we would have to keep even if it wasn't what he would most like to do. By handling his challenge this way, I preserved Dickie's sense of confidence and self-esteem. I didn't act like a raving giant who was going to force my will upon all the subjects in my kingdom! I had authority, and I used it. But I used it in a sensitive way that preserved his self-respect.

Bob, the father of a teen-age boy, described one of his struggles for power like this:

As Keith entered junior high, we were almost instantly confronted by his new need for independence. Our first confrontation came over my demand that he wear his new sweater to an evening youth meeting. Keith became very defiant and directly refused to wear the sweater—this was the first time he reacted to anything with defiance. I reacted very badly to his statement. I insisted that he *would* wear the sweater or he would spend the rest of the night in his room. Keith stalked into his room, slammed the door, and angrily stated he would stay in his room. I then realized how greatly this trivial matter had disturbed us both and ruined our evening. I went into Keith's room and told him how bad I felt and I knew he was disturbed also. He cried and agreed he was unhappy, so we discussed a solution to our problem. He agreed to wear his "windbreaker" to the meeting to alleviate my concern about his getting cold—and I agreed he would not be asked to wear a sweater which was really considered out of vogue for his peer group.

Both my experience with Dickie and Bob's with Keith are examples of a third way a child can learn to cope with his lack of confidence and power. He can have parents who neither let him run wild nor force him to rebel or become passive and dependent in an attempt to compensate for a lack of inner strength and confidence. In this solution we parents encourage our children's sense of individuality and uniqueness. We give them the opportunity to make many of their own decisions. We encourage them to speak up and express their feelings, and we come to mutual, cooperative solutions if at all possible. In other words, we value our children as important people and let them know that they can make a number of good decisions. We do not, however, let them draw us into a contest to see who will "win" and have his way.

When our children are very young, there may be relatively few situations where they can express their preferences and make their choices. These few center mostly around toys and play activities. As they grow older, however, our children can be encouraged to make their own choices about many matters. While there will always be times when we set limits, give directions, and say no, we will not overburden them with prohibitions. And when we do set standards and limits, we will do so thoughtfully and discuss them with the children. We will give them a chance to express their feelings even if they are negative. And we will listen and attempt to understand their perspective. When this happens, our children feel better even though they may not have their way. They know we respect them as persons and consider their feelings and desires.

Improving Your Child's Self-Confidence

For one reason or another, many children have a serious lack of confidence. Some children seem to be born this way. From the time we bring them home from the hospital they are overly sensitive. They don't eat well. They are colicky. They don't sleep soundly. And they are easily disturbed. While some children like to be cuddled and held, these children may stiffen when we attempt to hold them. As they get older they become either negative, critical, and hard to please—the power-oriented child—or outwardly anxious and insecure—the helpless-dependent controlling type. When this happens, we cannot say that anyone is to blame. Our children were different before we had a chance to mess them up! There were just some basic physiological differences.

In other cases a look at the family environment makes it clear why a child lacks confidence. There is little praise, excessive criticism, and an abundance of competition, conflict, and frustration. But whether our child was born predisposed to feelings of inferiority and a lack of confidence, or whether he has been trained to be that way (usually, of course, it is a combination of the two), we can take some very specific actions.

First and most important is *our own attitude.* We need to realize how important each of our children is to God and how our treatment of them will largely determine the attitudes they develop toward themselves. Although their physical

CONFIDENCE KILLERS

qualities, their playmates, their siblings, and their teachers will all influence their confidence, we the parents are the single most important determiners of our children's attitudes about themselves. We need to see our children's attitudes toward themselves as precious possessions. We need to realize how fragile their positive feelings are. And we need to see how beautifully they respond to our encouragement and sensitivity.

Criticism is probably the single biggest obstacle to developing self-confidence. When children are criticized, they lose confidence in themselves. They feel inadequate and feel like a failure. Even when we intend the criticism to be for their good (which we usually do), it can have a negative effect. I often tell parents it takes ninety-nine compliments to make up for one criticism! Whatever the ratio, I do know that most of us remember criticisms and "suggestions" long after we remember the positive things that others say about us.

Encouragement is a key to increasing children's self-confidence. We need to encourage our children to venture out and try new things. When they are afraid of failing, we may need to help them a bit at first. We can work with them and show them how something is done. Then, as soon as they begin to understand, we can step aside and let them try it for themselves. As in most situations, we tend to go to one of two extremes. Either we tell children to "go and do it"—without offering sufficient encouragement or making sure they know how to proceed—or we step in and do it for them. Between these two extremes is another option: helping and encouraging, but not doing it for the children.

Encouragement is closely related to *praise*. We need to take every opportunity to encourage our children and praise their efforts. They badly need and want our approval. Some of us find this difficult. Perhaps we were reared in homes where there was little encouragement and praise; maybe our own parents found it easier to criticize than to compliment. Whatever the reason, we have a hard time expressing words of encouragement and praise. We may even feel we are being dishonest if we compliment our children's efforts, since we see how they could have been improved.

This thought touches on a very sensitive point. We should not compliment insincerely. Children sense it if we routinely say "That's great" to everything they do. On the other hand, children need our praise even when the results of their efforts are imperfect. We need to achieve the sensitive balance that allows us always to sincerely appreciate their efforts and their accomplishments—no matter how feeble—if they have really tried. We should know what to expect from children our child's age. We should learn to compliment our children even though their work may not be up to our own standards. And when our children haven't really tried, we need to find out why not. It is likely that they are feeling inadequate and inferior and need a lot of building up.

Unfortunately, not all praise is helpful. A couple of years ago I was body-surfing at the beach, and I noticed nearby a man with a boy about Dickie's age. Every time the boy caught a wave, his father complimented him. He would say, "That's good!" or "That's great!" At first I was impressed. I thought, "It's great that father is complimenting his son on his surfing!" Then I noticed something interesting:

Every time the son came out of the water after catching a wave, he turned to his dad and asked, "How did I do, dad?" or "How was that?" In other words, his first thought was on the quality of his performance and his ability to please his father. Not once did he come out of the water and say, "That was a great one!" or "Boy, I sure enjoyed that one!" In complimenting his son, this father was unknowingly robbing the boy of doing something strictly for his own enjoyment. The surfing became another opportunity for the boy to please his father instead of to enjoy himself.

I don't share this little incident to warn parents who already have difficulty praising their children against the dangers of praise. Most of us need to learn to be much more expressive of our positive feelings. What I seek to show is that we should always keep in mind our children's need for a sense of *inner* satisfaction and enjoyment. When they are enjoying themselves and happy with their achievements, we should share their joy and fulfillment rather than calling attention to the performance aspects of their activities. We should say, "Hey, that looks like great fun!" or "You must have really enjoyed that one!" Comments like this show our children that we like to see them enjoying life, and this helps reduce the prevalent attitude in our society that performance is more important than inner feelings of satisfaction and contentment.

Parental worry and overprotection are two other attitudes that interfere with the development of our children's self-confidence. When we continually try to protect our children from all possible dangers or when we worry excessively about their safety or well-being, we are really saying, "I lack confidence in you. I don't think you can handle it." Or, "What if mama's little boy gets hurt?" These reactions plant feelings of doubt in our children's minds. Sometimes this becomes a major problem during adolescence. We would like to trust our teen-agers' driving, dating, work, and study habits. But partly because we remember our own adolescent experimentation and periodic irresponsibility and partly because of our children's past lapses and our awareness of the impact of peer pressure, we have trouble trusting. We warn, encourage, threaten, and remind them of potential pitfalls they may encounter as they begin to make their own decisions. So, in trying to help, we may actually undermine their confidence and push them toward the very activities we fear the most. Of course, we should communicate our concerns, but once or twice is usually enough. When we keep reminding our teens to "be careful" or "watch out," we are more likely to stir up resentment and undermine confidence than we are to help them be really careful.

Confidence and Teen-age Negativism

Many teen-agers go through a period of negativism, expressing an attitude that their parents can't do anything right. They argue at the slightest provocation. They criticize their parents' attitudes, their dress, their performance, and their friends. No matter what their parents do, it is never enough or it is "wrong" or "stupid." While a certain amount of this is normal, a serious problem can develop as a result of teen-agers' lack of confidence and their search for a sense of individuality

and identity. To the degree that they feel good about themselves and possess a firm inner sense of confidence and belonging, our teen-agers will not feel a need to put others down. But if they lack confidence, they will try to prove everyone else wrong in order to elevate themselves in their own and others' eyes.

An understanding of the reasons behind a teen-ager's negativism can help us handle it more wisely. Instead of fighting back, returning the criticism, or reprimanding our teen-agers for their attitudes, we can look beyond their admittedly negative behavior to their underlying fears and lack of confidence. When we see these inner feelings, we can be more sensitive to their struggles. We can encourage expression of their pent-up frustrations. We can see whether our own attitudes and actions are a part of the problem. And we can avoid "repaying evil with evil." As we do, we can find ways of building up our children's confidence and lessening the likelihood that they will misbehave out of a misguided search for power and control.

Chapter 6

IS YOUR CHILD "TOO GOOD"?

Most of us have been in the home of a perfectionistic home-maker. We arrive thirty minutes early for dinner, and she is there waiting for us. Everything is in its place. The table is set. The food is in the oven, and the kids are dressed and taken care of! At a time when most of us would be running around in a dither, she has everything under control. She has things so carefully scheduled that nothing can possibly go wrong. Even if we just "drop by," her house is in order. And she manages this with three children along with serving on a couple of committees at church or school!

Many men have similar personalities. We are workaholics. We are the first to arrive at work and the last to leave. We bring work home in the evenings and on weekends. When vacations roll around, we wonder whether we can get away. We think we are indispensable. And if we finally do manage to take a few weeks off, we very carefully plan the entire vaca-tion. We want to be sure we keep busy and don't get bored. We don't want to "waste time." Just sitting under a tree re-laxing feels strange. We become nervous because we are not busy. We get up and check the tent stakes. We drive to the nearest town and fill the car with gas. And we wonder if we shouldn't move on to another place. Unless we are busy, we become antsy. We want to get back home or to go to work or to move on to some new activities so we can feel we are accomplishing something.

This performance-oriented, perfectionistic style of life is so common in our society that we frequently fail to recognize it for what it is. In fact, this very style is often held out as a good example of the American ideal! But when we look beneath the surface of the perfectionist or the workaholic, we routinely find people with serious doubts about their significance and worth. Deep down they are not too sure of their own identity, so they have to work to be successful and try to prove their worth.

If people like this suffer a heart attack or in some other way are physically incapacitated, they invariably go into a very significant period of depression. Since their feelings of worth are tied up with their performance, they are suddenly taken aback. They have no true inner sense of worth because they have been relying on their performance for their identity. Now that they can't look at their day's performance and say, "Look at all I've done; I must be a valuable and significant person," they have little sense of value.

The perfectionistic and performance-oriented person is generally attempting to compensate for a third basic God-given need—the need for a sense of worth and value as a person. Whereas feelings of confidence relate to our ability to interact with others in a competent manner, feelings of worth relate more to our basic sense of value as a person. Although both a lack of confidence and a lack of worth may motivate us to excessive striving, their purposes are different. When we lack confidence we become competitive, power-oriented, or passive in order to control others and gain a sense of strength. When we lack feelings of self-worth, we attempt to achieve in order to demonstrate that we really are valuable, significant, or worthwhile.

A lack of worth may also lead to extreme efforts to be moral, good, or perfect. Superparents, for example, who try to do everything for their children and who get down on themselves if they can't live up to their image of an ideal parent, are often suffering from a lack of self-worth. By meeting every conceivable need of their children and by being the perfect parent, they hope to earn a sense of value as a person.

The Perfectionistic Child

Children lacking a deep inner sense of worth use the same strategies we adults do to overcome our lack of feelings of significance. Striving to please their parents and all others in authority, they are often among the top students in their class. They are extremely polite and likable. In fact, many parents would give anything if they had such well-behaved children! But beneath this externally well-behaved, cooperative, and achieving front, there may be young people who are really struggling with an inadequate sense of worth. Having serious reservations about themselves, they are continually at work proving their adequacy. Unfortunately this robs them of much of the freedom and happiness that should accompany the years of childhood.

These children are especially susceptible to guilt. When parents say, "Shame on you!" or "What is the matter with you?" or "Look what you've done now!" these children are deeply affected. Some almost wilt under this kind of criticism, crying or slinking off to their bedroom or another place of solace. Others do not evidence such obvious symptoms; they just "buck up and try harder." But their renewed efforts only serve to increase their inner pressure. They are developing a harsh inner taskmaster that continually pressures them to perform.

Upon reaching adolescence, these children typically move in one of two directions. Some continue their early patterns of self-inflicted pressure. Becoming overly involved in all sorts of school activities, they study for hours. They join every club

God-Given Need:	When Need Is Not Met:	Child Turns to Substitute of:
Worth	Unworthiness, Bad Behavior, Unimportance	Performance, Perfection

imaginable. And if they are active in their church, they are equally involved there.

At this point many parents become worried. They weren't bothered by the perfectionistic attitudes when their children were younger. But now the excesses of this style are becoming apparent. They are afraid their child may overdo it. And their concern is entirely justified. In fact, I have seen a number of teen-agers like this who eventually suffered "nervous breakdowns." They were under such pressure that they finally caved in. Many others grow into adulthood prone to guilt and feelings of discouragement and depression. They never learned to accept themselves no matter how superior their performance.

The Defeated Child

Other young adults growing up with perfectionistic standards take precisely the opposite tack. Having spent years "trying to be good," they are finally fed up. They have followed their parents' advice. They have followed their teachers' advice. And if they are Christians, they have sincerely attempted to follow God's will. They have attended Christian schools or camps. And partly because of their supersensitivity to their own failures, they have repeatedly confessed their sins. But their inner lack of a sense of worth makes it very difficult to really believe the Lord has forgiven them. They may temporarily relieve feelings of guilt by confessing their sins, but feelings of worthlessness soon rise up to erase their short-lived experience of forgiveness.

After repeated attempts at gaining inner peace by pleasing others, some of these adolescents eventually give up. Feeling it is useless to continue to seek a sense of self-worth through being good, they become burdened and depressed and begin resenting their parents, their teachers, their church leaders, and even God. Since they have repeatedly tried to please these people to no avail, they begin to feel that the whole system is unworkable. Their parents are unrealistic. Their teachers are insensitive. Their morality and work ethics are useless, and Christianity isn't all it's supposed to be. Consequently these young people throw off all their standards. Perfectionism and performance didn't get them what they wanted, so they will try the opposite. They may even decide the whole idea of sin and guilt simply drives people into depression and disappointment. If they are going to throw off their feeling of worthlessness, they must eventually reject the whole idea of God.

Students beginning college with these negative self-evaluations are especially susceptible to secular and humanistic emphases. They may take courses in psychology or philosophy in which the professor has negative attitudes toward religion and faith. Then they begin to read non-Christian authors who emphasize the fact that we should have positive self-concepts. Compared with their lifelong feelings of guilt, depression, and worthlessness, this new emphasis is exceedingly appealing. Rather than seeing how Christianity provides a solid foundation for self-acceptance and feelings of worth, they adopt a secular philosophy or lifestyle to meet their needs for worthiness. This is a tragic choice. Partly because of their emotional hang-ups, these young people end up rejecting the very faith that can provide them with what they need.

In summary, children lacking a sense of worth may be either "too good" or "too bad." In the first instance they try to be perfect to earn a sense of value they have not learned through their relationships with us. In the second they have given up trying!

Building Our Children's Sense of Worth

The starting place for instilling a deep sense of worth and value in our children is our attitude toward them. Most of us dearly love our sons and daughters and value them above almost everything else in life. Somehow, though, we get so busy with other things that we fail to communicate regularly how special they are to us; we assume that they should know how much we love and value them. But since children are in their formative years, we cannot make this assumption. Instead we should assume they hold very fragile feelings about themselves. Little failures, "helpful" criticisms, scoldings, and conflicts with peers can quickly undermine a young person's sense of self-esteem. We need to be aware of this and become the guardian of our children's self-worth and self-respect.

Sometimes our language undercuts our children's sense of worth and value. In various little ways we communicate disrespect or imply that they are not important "because they're children." This is well-illustrated in an article I read sometime ago. I cannot recall the source or the exact words, but the passage resembled the following:

> What if we talked to our friends the way we talk to our children? Our friends, Fred and Millie, would arrive for dinner and our conversation would go like this.
> "It's about time you got here, Fred. You're late again. . . . Well, come on in. Close the door. Were you born in a barn?"

"Sit down over here on the couch. Now remember, don't put your feet on the coffee table. You know what a fool you made of yourself the last time."

"O.K., let's eat. Everybody have a seat. Now you have to have a little bit of everything even if you don't like it. . . . Be careful with your drink, Fred. You know how clumsy you are. . . . No, you can't have dessert until you've cleaned up everything on your plate. And you're going to sit there until you are finished."

Needless to say, we would never speak to adult friends this way. But this is exactly the way many of us speak to our children day in and day out. We show more respect for friends and strangers than for our own children. We don't intend to, and we probably haven't even thought of our nagging and picking as disrespect. But when we think of talking to others the same way, it becomes obvious. We are really saying, "I don't trust you," "You are clumsy," "You are always late," and "You don't have sense enough to eat a decent meal."

I realize there may be some truth to these statements, since all children are at times clumsy, late, forgetful, and unreliable. And I also realize that you may feel as if your children are *always* this way! The truth is, much of this is normal and can be overcome with proper training. Proper training, however, does not consist of nagging, scolding, and subtly assassinating our children's character. These approaches only undermine their sense of worth and stir up more anger and resentment.

If we are going to instill a positive sense of self-worth in our children, we must learn to speak to them with deep respect. It is so easy to become angry and resort to name-calling, labeling, or character assassination. In a fit of anger, we may call one of our children "stupid," "lazy," or even "worthless." Even though we feel and express ourselves differently most of the time, these attacks make a deep impression. They tend to become a lasting part of our offspring's self-esteem and work against positive feelings of self-worth. This is especially true when we discipline our children.

If a child feels respected as a person when he is corrected, he will not lose respect for himself, though he may have done something very wrong. He will naturally feel bad about his mistake, but he will believe in himself that he can overcome the problem and do better next time. The child who does not feel respected when corrected will tend to despair when he does something wrong. He will not only fear the punishment, but be reawakened to the fact that he is nobody and bad. Instead of believing he can correct his problem, he will tend to be anxious or depressed or give up, perhaps feeling sorry for himself, saying, "I can never do anything right!"[1]

The story is told of a family that went out to dinner. The waitress asked the young boy of the family, "What would you like to eat, sonny?" "I'll have a hamburger," the boy replied proudly. But the mother looked sternly at the waitress and said, "He'll have the roast beef!"

Again directing her attention to the child, the waitress asked, "And what would you like on your hamburger?" "I'll have mustard and ketchup," the boy replied with a look of surprise. But once again the boy's mother interrupted and said, "He will have some green beans!"

Ignoring the mother, the waitress continued, "And what would you like to drink?" The little boy answered confidently, "I'll have a Coke!" The mother sternly said, "He will have some milk!"

The waitress left and in a few minutes returned with exactly what the little boy ordered. He looked at his mother in amazement and said, "Gee, mom. She thinks I'm real!"

This apocryphal story communicates a very important concept. All too often we parents treat our children as second-class citizens. Simply because they are children we may ignore their rights, their needs, and their opinions. We go on living in a world of adults, acting as though the world of children is somehow different and less important.

If we are going to help our children develop a full apprecia-

---

[1]Maurice Wagner, *The Sensation of Being Somebody* (Grand Rapids: Zondervan Publishing House, 1975), p. 78.

tion of their significance and worth, we must begin by valuing their ideas and opinions. Nothing tells a person he is more important than to have someone listen to his ideas and value them as important. Whether it regards the choice of a dress, the food we eat, the color of the new car, the best professional football player, the best church, or some political issue, children need a chance to voice their opinions and know that they are heard.

By listening to our children's values and interests, we are telling them they are valuable people who are worth listening to. When we neglect their ideas, take strong opposition to them, or use timeworn phrases like "You will understand when you grow up" or "You are just a child and you wouldn't understand," we are really telling our children their ideas are not good enough to be taken into consideration. Although our children may not have the maturity to make the best decisions, we do need to solicit their opinions and bring them into our discussions as much as possible. When we do, we lay a foundation for a lasting sense of self-worth and self-esteem.

I remember when we used to be a one-car family. Kathy and the children would pick me up in the afternoon. I would climb into the driver's seat with Kathy next to me, and the children would have to sit in back. I would say hi to the kids, give them a big hug, and begin a conversation with Kathy. We talked about her activities and my day. Rarely did we speak directly to our children. They were supposed to sit quietly in the back as we discussed "important" matters. Typically they would sit there for a few minutes and then begin to fuss or fight. Finally we realized what was happening. In failing to include Dickie and Debbie in our communication, we were actually telling them they were not important. Their thoughts and their wishes and their reports about their day would have to wait until mom and dad were finished. The trouble was, mom and dad usually did not finish until we were safely at home and ready for dinner. And even then we usually continued to monopolize the conversation!

When we saw what we were doing, we started bringing them into the conversation from the very first. We asked them about their day. And when we discussed my work or Kathy's activities, we tried to do it in ways that the children could understand and participate in. Although it took a little time to break our old habits, we soon learned we could really enjoy our children on these occasions. We are also confident they feel like a much more integral part of our family and of much more significance and value than they would if we had continued our one-sided conversations. Besides that, they fight less while riding in the car!

Another way to increase children's sense of self-worth is to bring them into family planning. By this I mean the whole process of decision making in the home. If we are like most parents, we have a tendency to sit down with our mate, discuss a situation, arrive at a decision, and then inform the children. While this is certainly proper at times, there are other situations when we all can profit from mutual discussions.

A couple of years ago our family decided it was time to purchase a new car. I had a couple of models in mind, but they weren't exactly what Kathy was thinking of! She felt we needed a station wagon so we could comfortably transport the entire family, the groceries, and the several other odds and ends that find their way into the family vehicle. I wanted an economy car. We talked it over and began our shopping. Each time we looked at a new car, we had Dickie and Debbie try out the back seats, since that is where they would be spending a great deal of their time. They told us whether the leg room was adequate or too tight. They checked out the storage space behind the back seat because a lot of their equipment would have to fit there. And they gave their opinions about color and other issues. After looking at several dealers and trying several models, we finally came to a mutual decision. The car was slightly larger than I had planned, yet slightly smaller than Kathy had originally hoped for. It also had plenty of room for two children and a variety of things in the back seat. We came away feeling we had made a good decision—and we had made it as a family. We all know we played an important role in the selection.

Discussions about car purchases are just one of hundreds of topics our children should be involved in. From the meals we eat to the clothes our children purchase and wear, our leisure activities, the new furniture (especially if it is for the children's use), our vacation plans, and the restaurant we are going to visit, we have an abundance of opportunities for involving our children in family planning.

If we take time to talk things over, we can nearly always arrive at a solution that takes everybody's wishes into consideration. By bringing our children into family planning we tell them they are important. We tell them we value their ideas. And we tell them we think they are significant, important people. This has to have a positive effect on their feelings of self-worth, and it promotes a much more cooperative attitude among our children.

I should emphasize at this point that I am not suggesting we abdicate our parental responsibility and turn the decision making over to the children. I am also not suggesting we operate on the basis of a democracy or the "one man, one vote rule" that some psychologists propose. I am suggesting a loving leadership where we adults respect our children, value their thoughts, wishes, and feelings, and involve them in our family's planning.

There are times when we may leave a decision entirely up to the children. There are times when we will make the decision. And there may be times when we "vote." Each of these have their place. The key issue is our willingness to involve our children. When we do this, they won't try to run everything and make all the decisions. In fact, as they grow older they will have less need to rebel and reject our values, because they will have good feelings about themselves and their decision-making abilities.

It is children whose parents do not respect their opinions

and who fail to bring them into family planning in their younger years who often turn against their parents in adolescence. Since they have never had a chance to make their own decisions, they feel they must rebel to find their own identity and prove that they can function on their own. When children have been brought up sharing their opinions and participating in family planning, they have a much easier time making the transition from the dependency of childhood to the independency of adulthood. Consequently their adolescent years are much easier for all.

Chapter 7

"I'M BORED!"

One Saturday afternoon I was working at our dining room table when all of a sudden something caught my eye outside the window. Our son was marching back and forth with a two-by-three-foot picket sign. In big, bold letters he had written "I AM BORED!" When Dickie knew he had my attention, a huge smile spread across his face. I began to laugh, and so did he. After calling Kathy over to view our "labor-management" problems, I dropped my work and went outside to talk with our "picket."

"Dad," Dickie said, "I'm bored." I gave him a big hug, told him how cute his sign was, and said, "Let's go inside and talk this over." After a little discussion, Dickie and I decided to go downtown for a soft drink and check out a new restaurant I was thinking of taking Kathy to.

Sometimes Dickie and Debbie are not so cute when they are bored. In fact, they are more likely to start fighting when they are bored than at any other time.

Boredom is a common cause of our children's misbehavior. It is caused by a lack of constructive activity to occupy our children, and it results in a search for alternative activities,

God-Given Need:	When Need Is Not Met:	Child Turns to Substitute of:
Constructive Activity	Boredom	Attention

frequently of a disturbing or destructive nature. Along with needs for love, confidence, and worth, our children also need interesting activities to challenge them and occupy their time. When God placed Adam and Eve in the Garden of Eden, He didn't tell them to go twiddle their thumbs, play in the street, or leave Him alone! Instead, He got them busy. He told Adam to name the animals, and he instructed Adam and Eve to populate the earth and have dominion over it. He planned enough to keep them occupied.

Few things can drive a parent to the brink of despair more quickly than a bored child. Nearly every mother (and many fathers) can testify to the utter frustration they have felt in trying to cope with continual interruptions, fights, and hassles growing out of the children's boredom. As one father put it: "When my children keep whining 'What can I do?' I feel like screaming! I could tell them one hundred things to do and they still would not be satisfied!"

Good Days and Bad

Most families have their good days and their bad. Almost like clockwork, Saturdays can be expected to go well in certain families; in other households, Saturdays are miserable times but Sundays are O.K. Some parents find weekdays are generally happy times; for others, weekends are best. Most of us even find that certain hours of the day are better than others. Don't you find that you can almost predict when your children will be in trouble? For some reason every family develops its own rhythm or style. Based on our schedules and habits and personal styles, we are able to get along better on certain days and at certain times than others.

One of the big contributors to this cycle is our children's boredom. Some families find Saturdays are horrible because there is nothing going on that interests the children. Television occupies them for a few hours in the morning, but eventually that gets tiring. And since we are often busy with our own activities, our children can easily become bored and feel left out. When this stage is reached, we had better have some plans in mind unless we want trouble. In fact, it is best to plan our weekends so these times never arrive. Similarly, if our children tend to get bored and upset at a predictable time in the afternoon, it may help to sit down and find out why. Have they already exerted the stock of energy they have for planning new activities? Are they tired of playing with their brothers and sisters? Are they tired of being left out of our "adult" activities? Or are they tired of the routine of school? Whatever the specific cause, a little reflection makes it possible to help them plan some interesting activities. And this planning will prevent many problems and conflicts.

Early in our family life I assumed Dickie and Debbie should be responsible for finding ways to occupy their time. "Kathy and I are busy," I thought, "and the children ought to be able to think of things they would like to do." But although my assumption made a lot of sense to me, I found that our children didn't seem to work that way. Periodically they would say "I'm bored" or "What can I do?" If I offered a suggestion, they were likely to reject it or to go about their way for a few minutes only to return again and repeat their question—this time with a bit more force. At first this was irritating to me. I was busy and didn't want to be bothered. Besides that, it seemed as if whatever I suggested, our children didn't want to do it!

Finally I thought the situation through with Kathy. We talked about the way we felt when we were bored. We realized that when we were bored, some little suggestion wouldn't help us either. Boredom, at least for us, required more drastic measures. We decided that if this was true of us, it might also be true of our children. So we discussed what it took to get us out of periods of boredom. Usually it was people! And if it wasn't people, it was some really stimulating activity, not simply reading a book, watching another television program, or playing with our toys.

Realizing this, we decided to try to stop whatever we were doing long enough to sit down with our children, allow them to express their feelings of boredom or dissatisfaction, and really see what we could do to help. We quickly found they responded positively to this approach. Behind the statement "I am bored" they were often carrying another message. This one read, "Will you spend some time with me? I am lonely!" or "I feel left out." Once we learned to interpret our children's underlying message, we were off and running. Now we can usually help them out of their boredom with just a few minutes of well-spent time and planning. And if the problem calls for a bigger solution, we will occasionally plan something really significant like a Dodger baseball game, a shopping trip, or the children's favorite restaurant.

Kathy is great at these solutions. She loves to plan things ahead of time so she can look forward to them. Each week she does a bit of informal planning for and with the family. She thinks through the children's activities and our own. If Dickie and Debbie have plenty of activities, she lets it go at that. But if she senses they may not have much time with friends in the ordinary course of the week, she will encourage them to invite a friend over some afternoon or evening, or she will suggest we plan a night out or set up a family evening. In this way we all have something to look forward to. There is an activity to break up the routine, to be enjoyed, and to make everyone feel special. We have learned that this kind of planning heads off many problems that would otherwise arise from boredom and routine.

On weekends and holidays we also try to plan ahead. Many times there is plenty going on. School functions, soccer games, invitations to friends' homes, swimming, or just neighborhood play times will keep everyone occupied. But if we sense things are likely to go slow by midafternoon, we may talk it over with Dickie and Debbie and discuss something we can do together. The activity is inconsequential; the important thing is that we find something the entire family enjoys. We all need to become sensitive to our children's needs for interesting activities. When our children are left alone at times like this, we should expect trouble to begin. They will probably start repeatedly interrupting, arguing, picking a fight, or finding some other way to stir up a little action.

Sometimes parents ask me, "What should we do with the child who is constantly climbing the walls?" If I want to play "crystal ball reader," I reply, "Is he two, and do you live in an apartment?" Parents are amazed at my great insight, but the truth is really very simple! What two-year-old who is cooped up in an apartment wouldn't be climbing the walls? A child like that is not maladjusted, and he doesn't need correction. He is bored stiff in his limited environment and needs to get out of the house. He needs a place to run and play. He needs some friends. And he needs some physical activity. Unless and until he gets these things, he is going to be a "problem child"!

Teen-agers react to boredom in a slightly different way. Sometimes they mope around trying to make everyone else share their misery. Often, however, they seek out their friends and begin looking for stimulating activities. Unfortunately, "stimulating" often means trying something new, taking a chance, or pushing the limits of good judgment, parents, or society. Reckless driving, pranks, and experimenting with alcohol and drugs are all fair game for the bored teen-ager who is looking for an exciting substitute for constructive activity. Because of the strong tendency for teen-agers to seek out dangerous experiences to ward off boredom, it is crucial that we do everything in our power to see that they have a variety of healthy and challenging activities and friends. An active church youth group with a number of sharp peers is one of the best ways to combat this potential problem.

Parents Need Time Too

In the past several chapters I have pointed out the urgency of spending a great deal of quality time with our children. Do not misunderstand: I am not suggesting that every time our children utter a peep, we drop what we are doing and run to their sides. We should not be servants at our children's beck and call. We should not let them constantly interrupt our activities. And we should never train them to think that they should never have to wait.

There are times when it is impossible to stop what we are doing and enter into an activity with our children. There are other times when it is not wise to do so. If we do not train our children properly, they will fail to realize that other people have rights too.

My point is this: Parents generally do not structure either their day or their children's day in ways that give them and the children a lot of quality time together. Instead, we tend to go our way until there is a problem. A much better way is to plan ahead and help our children find enjoyable activities and times of mutual pleasure.

An hour or so spent in planning and playing with our children each day can actually allow us to get more of our own work done around the house. If we add up the amount of time we spend correcting our children, stopping fights, and handling interruptions, it will probably amount to a good bit more than an hour. On top of that, the anxiety and frustration cast a cloud over everything else we are trying to accomplish. But if we take time to single out our children, focus on them, and help them to plan their days, they will be much less likely to interrupt and cause us hassles.

I suggest a three-step plan when children interrupt us to complain of "nothing to do" or show other signs of being bored. First, we should stop and see if there really is a problem. We must understand our children's feelings from their perspective: if we were in their shoes, would we be bored too?

Then we should hear the children out, let them express their feelings, and help them find something that stimulates their interest. Since boredom is often associated with feelings of being left out or alone, the best suggestions sometimes include things we can do together.

Years ago I was working on a manuscript at our dining room table. Dickie, just a few years old, asked with an imploring look on his face, "Daddy, will you play with me?" Being engrossed in my work, I gave him a little hug and said "Not now. Dad's busy right now." A few minutes later, Dickie was back again. Once again he asked if I would play with him. I was right in the middle of a chapter and didn't appreciate being interrupted. Irritated, I started to say, "Can't you see I'm busy? I'm writing a book telling parents how to love their children." Then I realized that I was putting my work ahead of my son, so I put down my pen and said, "Dickie, let's go downtown for a Coke." He lit up as we jumped into the car and drove to a nearby fast food restaurant. We were gone less than forty minutes, but when we came home, Dickie immediately ran off to occupy himself on his own and I returned to my work.

That was perhaps the best forty minutes I ever spent! Dickie was happy; I had a pleasant experience with him; and I had no more interruptions! Taking action like this is the second step in helping our sons and daughters overcome their boredom.

If we are convinced our children have plenty of appealing things to do or if we just cannot be interrupted at the moment, we can take a third step. We can stop our work momentarily, look them in the eye, give them our full attention, hear their complaint, and tell them when we can help or why we cannot. We might say, "I know you are feeling bored, honey, and I would like to help. But right now I just can't drop what I am doing. In a half-hour I should be finished, and then we can have some time together."

Sometimes, of course, our children are just too demanding. This is especially true of younger children who have naturally short attention spans and lack the resources to plan their own activities. As one mother put it:

> What do you do after you have spent time with a child and you have to get your work done? My son is two and continually wants attention. I read him a story, give him love, and then explain that I am busy. He continues to want attention and nag me. It seems like children are basically selfish and want more attention than one can give!

Many of us can identify with this mother's concern. We have encountered nearly identical situations. And much that she says is true. Our children often do want more attention than we can give. When this happens, we need to be sure we are doing all we can to play with them and keep them busy. Sometimes another child will occupy their time. Sometimes television will serve as a short-term electronic baby sitter. Or sometimes a newspaper to cut up will help!

When we have done all we can, we have to let them know clearly that we cannot spend any more time with them for a specific period of time. After that we will ignore their interruptions or, if they become destructive or obnoxious, lovingly but firmly send or take them to their rooms. This way we are taking them seriously and letting them know that we want to help and we will as soon as we have time. When our children learn we will keep our word and aren't just putting them off, they will usually find some way to get by until we are free.

Chapter 8

THE SEARCH FOR REVENGE AND SAFETY

A young couple once stopped me after a meeting to discuss a problem with their children. They were recently married, and it was the second marriage for the wife. Although it had been more than two years since her first marriage ended, Mark, her oldest child, was not getting along with his stepfather at all. The stepfather showed a great deal of sensitivity to the children; he was not forcing himself on them. But no matter what he did, Mark reacted negatively. He refused to go places with his stepfather. He refused to say more than a few words. And in general, he was nasty.

As we talked the situation over, it was apparent that Mark saw his stepfather as an intruder and was blaming him for his parents' breakup. His negativism and rejection of his stepfather was his way of expressing his hostility and gaining revenge for the hurt he had suffered.

In Genesis we are told another story of family conflict.

> Joseph, a young man of seventeen, was tending the flocks with his brother, . . . and he brought his father a bad report about them. Now Israel loved Joseph more than any of his other sons, because he had been born to him in his old age;

and he made a richly ornamented robe for him. When his
brothers saw that their father loved him more than any of
them, they hated him and could not speak a kind word to him
(Gen. 37:2–4).

Joseph's tattling, a couple of his dreams, and his father's
favoritism combined to stir up his brothers' resentment. They

became so angry that they plotted to kill him. They decided they could murder Joseph, toss him into a well, and tell their father a wild animal had attacked and eaten him. Fortunately Joseph's oldest brother, Reuben, offered an alternative. He suggested they simply throw Joseph into the well alive— apparently with the idea of his returning later to rescue him. About this time the brothers noticed a caravan coming on its way to Egypt and decided to sell Joseph as a slave. This way they wouldn't suffer the guilt of murder and would have twenty pieces of silver for their efforts!

Mark's rejection of his stepfather and the scheming of Joseph's brothers were both motivated by a desire for revenge. This is a fifth common cause of our children's misbehavior. When their needs for love, confidence, worth, and construc- tive activity go unmet or are attacked or undermined, our children tend to become resentful and seek ways to get even with whoever has undercut their emotional balance. Along with misbehaving to gain attention, for example, children who feel unloved are also likely to become angry at the one from whom they desire love. To get even, they will find ways of punishing that person for not loving them properly.

Similarly, children lacking confidence may get into re- peated power struggles both to try to prove their strength and to make life miserable for their parents. When children lack a sense of worth, they may turn to perfectionistic behavior. But they may also give up entirely. By quitting, they gain revenge on the parents for their failure to make them feel a positive sense of inner worth. The children think, "Since they think I am no good I may as well live up to their expectations. That will show them." And when children become bored for lack of constructive activity, they will often get into trouble both to occupy their time and to tell mom or dad "if you don't help me find something to do, I will make you regret it!"

The desire to gain revenge is at the root of most of our children's feelings of anger and frustration. In fact, revenge is perhaps the primary motivating force behind all anger. When

God-Given Needs	When Needs Go Unmet	Child Turns to Revenge

someone hurts us, either physically or emotionally, we want to even the score and see them suffer a little in return! This is one reason why children slam the door when they are sent to their room for discipline. It is one reason why they stick out their tongue, make a face, or sass us. And it is one reason why they make a scene when we force them to go with us against their will. They know that their negative reactions will upset us, and that is precisely what they intend!

The search for revenge wears a thousand disguises. Teen-agers whose parents are committed Christians may rebel against their Christian training in order to express deep feelings of resentment. Some teen-age girls become pregnant out of wedlock to spite their parents. Many children do poorly at school to irritate and upset their parents. And most young children get into a variety of messes to tell their parents "you had better spend more time with me . . . or else!" Anytime our children evidence a regular pattern of hostility or negativism, we need to ask ourselves with whom they feel a need to get even and why. Then we can start addressing the

real problem—whatever is undermining their feelings of belonging, confidence, or worth.

The Search for Psychological Safety

Anytime our children feel unloved, incompetent, unworthy, or bored they begin doing things to ward off these uncomfortable feelings. I call this a search for psychological safety. In addition to turning to attention, power, perfectionism, and substitute activities, they also find other ways of coping with their inner hurt. They may simply begin to *with-draw*. Since they feel unloved, inadequate, or unworthy, they are afraid to get involved with the neighborhood children. Because they are extremely sensitive to criticism and rejection, they keep to themselves. They play alone. They have few friends. And they are generally shy and quiet.

Those of us who are not this way often have difficulty understanding this type of child. We encourage them to "go out and make some friends," "speak up," or "be more aggressive." We try to tell them that if they don't want to be bored or lonely, they need to "go out and play with the other kids." Our proddings seem entirely logical. If people don't want to feel lonely, they should get involved with others. But it is precisely because withdrawn children feel unloved or lack confidence and a sense of worth that they don't get involved. Fearing further rejection, they believe it is safer to be alone. Their withdrawal, in other words, is designed to provide them with a sense of psychological safety. It is intended to make them feel less unloved, incompetent, or unworthy.

Giving up is a closely related way of coping with feelings of incompetence or worthlessness. Some children feel so badly about themselves that they just quit trying. Failure is so overwhelming, they cannot risk it, so they avoid even attempting something. This is the only way they know to protect their fragile feelings.

Repression is another technique children use to avoid feeling bad about themselves. By repression we mean the attempt to put unpleasant memories or feelings out of awareness. Thoughts or feelings that are unpleasant or would bring about criticism, anger, or disapproval are pushed into our child's unconscious. Have you noticed, for example, how nearly all very young children—let's say up to two years of age—tend to be spontaneous, free, alive, and happy? They generally let us know their thoughts, desires, or feelings. We don't have to ask a two-year-old how he is feeling; he will spontaneously show his anger and frustration or his enjoyment and excitement. But in our society, parents and others soon let children know what is acceptable and what is not. We teach young boys that "men don't cry." In scores of ways we communicate disapproval of certain attitudes and actions. Sometimes we scold our children for excitedly running into the room and sharing a great thing that just happened when we are talking with a friend. Sometimes we tell them, "It is not right to be angry." And sometimes we tell them, "Don't be too excited." In every instance we are encouraging them to restrain themselves and hide or at least suppress the spontaneity and expression of their feelings.

A certain amount of this is necessary. Children need to learn that they cannot interrupt for every little thing. They need to learn to handle their emotions of anger and resentment constructively. But sometimes we as parents go too far. We punish, criticize, shame, or in some other way voice our disapproval of normal emotional reactions. The message our children receive is not "Enjoy your feelings appropriately." Instead they hear, "Don't have those feelings!" or "Don't be so spontaneous!" Some parents even tell their children, "Christians shouldn't feel *that* way!" Somewhat confused and bewildered because they *do* feel that way, all our children can do is feel that they are somehow bad. Since this is painful, they gradually learn to push their feelings out of consciousness. Although the feelings are still lying there somewhere in their mental life, the children are no longer aware of them. They become more controlled, less spontaneous, and in general a little less sensitive to their own emotions. They do this to find a sense of safety.

This repression can cause serious problems. Children who are afraid to express their feelings are more prone to develop psychosomatic problems like ulcers, headaches, and lower back pains. They also have difficulties in marriage, where openness and honesty about feelings is important. Sometimes they grow up almost devoid of conscious feelings; they operate, as one person put it, with "refrigerators for hearts and

computers for brains!" And if they don't have severe problems, they nevertheless suffer from a loss of spontaneity or
have occasional surprising and destructive outbursts of their
usually hidden emotions.

Reaction formation is another defense children use to
maintain a sense of psychological safety. In reaction formation
we adopt a conscious attitude that is exactly the opposite of
our true inner feelings. If we have strong feelings of anger, for
example, we may become very loving, kind, and patient,
hiding the fact that we really have a good bit of hostility.
Children do this because they are afraid of expressing their
anger for fear of reprisal or punishment. But this mechanism
can be carried to extremes. Children who are always nice and
never angry are a lot like the perfectionistic ones who think
they must always perform perfectly to be accepted. *Nobody* is
without some negative emotions—especially a young child.

When I see a young child who is always nice, I get a little
worried. Children can be nice and polite for two reasons.
They can be nice because they feel good about themselves
and others and are spontaneously affectionate and kind. Or
they can be nice because they are just too fearful to be otherwise! Early in life they learned that angry feelings were not
acceptable, so they developed a style of life that was exactly
the opposite to ensure they would not lose their parents' approval. Like children who repress their emotions, these children are likely to grow up out of touch with their true feelings. They may even go on crusades against people who show
the very traits they had hidden in their own lives!

I once counseled a minister with this problem. He spent a
lot of time preaching the evils of alcohol, drugs, and sex. But
when he had an emotional breakdown, he started drinking
heavily and chasing women. Since he had never admitted his
own temptations, he had been unable to learn to cope with
them constructively. Now, under the pressure of his emotional breakdown, his previously repressed feelings started to
control his life.

Rationalization is another mechanism we use to protect our sense of psychological safety. In this defense we simply think up a thousand reasons to explain why we really were not at fault. If our team lost, it was because of the umpire. If we received a low grade in deportment, it was because we were sitting next to someone who "talks all the time." If we failed to finish some chore, it was because "we had too much to do." The excuses are endless, but their purpose is consistent. In all ways, at all costs, we let someone know that we were innocent so we cannot be blamed.

This is obviously a universal human tendency. We all try to make excuses to put ourselves in a good light. But we usually don't stop to understand what is behind our rationalizing. Is it not the fear that others will blame us, criticize us, or condemn us? In other words, if we acknowledge our failures, then our feelings of acceptance, confidence, or worth would be attacked. Just as we withdraw from some situations to avoid feelings of worthlessness, loneliness, or failure—and just as we repress other feelings to avoid the pain of rejection or disesteem—we rationalize other failures to avoid these same negative emotions.

Overcompensation is another way of attempting to ensure our sense of psychological well-being. We have probably all known people who were limited in one area of talent and worked hard to make up for it in another. Perhaps they were not good students, but spent hours "working out" in the gym. They lifted weights, shot baskets, ran for miles, or in other ways drove themselves until they excelled in athletics. Others who do not feel accepted socially may turn to academics to compensate for their negative self-evaluations. They throw themselves into their studies. They do homework every night. They take on self-study projects. And they become straight A students.

The star athlete and the top student reap the admiration of people for the most part. But have you ever noticed that sometimes they become very one-sided? The athlete works so hard in one area that he fails to develop other aspects of his personality. Perhaps he fails to develop intellectually. The "scholar" fails to develop in his social life. And often, even after these people have excelled, they continue to feel inadequate. All their accolades and achievements have given them only temporary relief from their underlying feelings of inferiority and lack of self-esteem.

We could list other methods children use to hide their underlying lack of confidence, love, and worth. But this brief survey should be enough to show how the general process works. Psychologists usually call these processes "psychological defense mechanisms." I am calling them ways of searching for psychological safety because their major purpose is to ward off uncomfortable inner emotions and provide an inner feeling of psychological health.

A sensitivity to these safety techniques in our children helps us to see when they are hurting emotionally. Rather than trying to correct or discipline them, we can try to understand the feelings that are causing them to try to hide their inner hurt. Then we can take action to meet their underlying needs and address their real problems. This is one of the best ways of helping them give up unnecessary safety mechanisms.

Part 3

WHAT NEXT?

Chapter 9

ISN'T ANYTHING NORMAL?

By now you may be wondering if your children ever do anything without some hidden reason! Are all their problem behaviors caused by the search to fulfill unmet needs, or do some of them "just happen"? Please rest assured that not all our own children's troubling reactions are motivated by our failure to meet their needs for love, confidence, worth, and activity. This is a major cause, but not the only one. Moreover, it is important to understand a few of the other causes in order to train our children effectively. That is our goal in this chapter.

Most of the problems we will discuss here should not really be called misbehaviors, since they are normal reactions growing out of our children's level of physical and emotional maturity. But since they often cause hassles for us as parents, we will use the term "misbehavior" loosely to describe them.

Eating Problems

Probably the first "misbehavior" or problem parents face with young children is how to motivate them to eat. Many children are born finicky, and most have some very strong culinary dislikes. Along with these picky tastes we are likely to encounter minor tantrums at mealtimes—cups and plates knocked over, and a variety of utensils sent sailing to the floor! Although all these reactions are completely normal, I think you will agree that they are also serious problems—at least for the parents. So let's look at the causes of these problems and see what—if anything—we can do.

Can you imagine for a moment that you are a relatively young infant—perhaps about six or nine months? For most of your young life you have enjoyed either your mother's milk or a satisfying substitute. One day your mother decides to introduce you to another kind of food. Instead of being smooth and liquid, it is soft and mushy. It has a different and unfamiliar aroma and taste. If your mother is extremely fortunate, you may happen to like this new experience. But most likely you will not like it. If you are a Slow-to-Warm-Up Child, your first reaction is to turn up your nose, pucker your lips, and spit the food out! You have absolutely no thought of misbehaving, not cooperating, or being a bad child. You are simply doing what comes naturally—spitting out something you can't stand! Your mother, however, doesn't see it this way! She wants you to grow up nice and healthy. She wants to expand your tastes. And she doesn't want to spend the rest of her life nursing you. So, since your desires and your mother's are at odds, you have a problem that must be solved.

Some mothers would try to manipulate you into eating foreign food. If yours is in a good mood, she smiles and plays a game like "airplane." She puts a bite on a spoon and with a big sweeping motion gleefully proclaims "coming in for a landing." But not to be fooled, you recognize the stuff and spit it out again! Or perhaps mother decides to use the power approach. Since she is bigger than you, she tries to force it down your throat. She puts a heavy thumb on one side of your jaw and her middle finger on the other and forces you to open up! As soon as you do, she crams it in. But not to be outdone, you quickly spit it out! Needless to say, this whole scene is hard on everyone concerned and not the best way to handle this little problem.

Another approach is to tell you, "O.K. If you don't eat it, you'll starve!" This approach may be fine when you become a little older, but at this age you aren't old enough to understand, so you happily go your way, not realizing that your mother is going to refuse to feed you the next time you are hungry. And when she does, you have already forgotten the last fiasco and haven't the foggiest notion why she won't feed you! Once again, this approach will seldom come to a happy conclusion.

The best solution is for your parents to recognize that children have limited tastes. Rather than forcing new and strange-tasting foods down your throat, they should respect your tastes the same way they would like others to respect theirs. They should introduce you to new foods, but take it easy and do it gradually. Can you imagine how you would feel as an adult if your wife said, "I don't care if you like it or not. You are going to eat it!" Although you might try to accommodate yourself somewhat to her culinary selections, you would also like the right to voice your own opinions. After all, you're the one who has to eat it!

The point of this discussion on eating is this: It is entirely normal for young children to have limited appetites, and we should not force them to eat things they detest! Rather than looking at their rejection of food as rebellion, disobedience, or stubbornness, we should see it for what it is—an entirely normal dislike for certain foods. And rather than seeing this as an opportunity to discipline our children, we should give them time to mature and learn to accept new experiences.

This does not mean that after children leave the bottle and begin eating solid foods, they have the right to demand whatever they are in the mood for. In fact, this is one of the quickest ways to spoil children. I suggest that we try to fix at least one dish every family member likes and leave it to them whether or not to eat it. If we have several finicky eaters, we may fix a salad that one of them likes, a main dish that another likes, and a dessert that the other one prefers. This will ensure that no one starves. And once children learn they can have no snacks between meals unless they have eaten a decent meal, they will begin to broaden their tastes a bit.[1]

Temptations for Toddlers

When our children reach the toddler stage, most of us encounter another problem. Normal, healthy, inquisitive children like to get into everything in sight! Newspapers, magazines, vases, and family heirlooms are all fair game for the toddler. Some parents take their toddlers' explorations as misbehavior. They believe their children are being rebellious and disobedient and thus they should take this opportunity to teach them to respect other people's property and follow orders. They expect that once they have told children to leave something alone, they will leave it alone. And if they do not, they should be spanked. As one father put it, "A one-or-two-year-old must be taught he can't touch things, just as we adults can't touch certain things. If they don't learn it then, they never will!" While some parents have followed this direction without inflicting psychic scars on their children, I believe there is a better way. This way follows logically from an understanding of why a toddler continually gets into everything in sight.

Once again, we need to put ourselves in our children's shoes. Imagine that we are only a year old or so and were placed in a strange world of people and objects we had never seen. As soon as we were old enough to move around a bit, we would want to explore our world. We would want to touch things, put them in our mouth. tear them up, and do everything we could to find out how they work and how they feel. In fact, if we did not have this interest, we would probably be a very lethargic or listless baby, and our parents should be

---

[1]Chapter 5 of my book *Help! I'm a Parent* (Grand Rapids: Zondervan, 1972) deals specifically with what to do with a finicky eater.

concerned! Our inquisitiveness is a healthy aspect of growing up. We are beginning to use our intelligence to understand and explore our world!

If, in the middle of exploring this new world, our giant parent comes along and sternly says no and gives us a swat, we immediately have a feeling of being bad or doing something wrong. The parent's correction, in other words, turns our exploration into a moral issue. Our natural inquisitiveness is checked by the feeling that it is bad or wrong. If we were a couple of years older, this would pose no problem; we would be able to comprehend the necessity of leaving things alone, not breaking mother's china, and respecting other people's property. But at this stage of our life we are just not mentally capable of comprehending the situation. And if we are really curious, we have a special problem. Even if our parents discipline and threaten us, we are drawn almost irresistibly to some forbidden objects!

The apostle Paul penned a verse that I believe has a truly practical application to this problem. He said, "God . . . will not let you be tempted beyond what you can bear. But when you are tempted, he will also provide a way out so that you can stand up under it" (1 Cor. 10:13). If we look at God as a model parent, we find an important principle here. We should not tempt our children more than they can bear. And when they are tempted, we should also make a way of escape. I suggest that leaving a variety of interesting objects within the reach of toddlers is tempting them above what they are able to bear! As an alternative, I suggest "kiddie proofing" our homes while we have young children. As much as possible, we should move our valuable and breakable objects to a higher level. By the time our children reach three years of age or so they will be able to understand why they should leave things alone, and we can put back the objects and discipline if the children get into things they shouldn't. In the meantime, let's not tempt them. And if we must have a few forbidden items within their reach, we should be sure not only to tell

them what they cannot play with, but also to give them a way out. Show them interesting substitutes, or turn their attention to other things.

Sanity While Shopping

Closely related to curiosity and exploration around the house is the way our young children carry on in the market while we are shopping. If our children are normal, it is likely that they will begin asking for things the moment they walk in the door. They walk up and down the aisles taking things off the shelves, they push the shopping cart wildly down the aisle, throw a tantrum when they cannot have their way, or create some other kind of disturbance. Once again, this is entirely normal behavior but definitely a problem. Like eating conflicts and curiosity, however, these problems among young children are not caused by some unmet emotional needs—unless, perhaps, our child is suffering from boredom, which may compound this problem.

To understand why children often have trouble on shopping trips, let's put ourselves in their shoes again. Imagine walking into this huge store with your giant parent. You are intrigued with the great variety of interesting things—many of which you have seen on television! As you go up and down the aisles, your giant parent takes goods off the shelves and puts them into the cart one after the other. Everything mother wants, she gets. You, on the other hand, can't have anything you want! Every time you point or ask or grab for something, she tells you no and keeps on going. Before long, this gets a little tiring! You have nothing to do, can make no choices, and have to watch her get everything she wishes. Now, what normal child wouldn't get a little tired of this?

One of the best ways of handling this situation is to find some way of involving our children in the shopping. If they are old enough, we can send them off to pick up a few items on our list. We might also let them select a thing or two. If we need dry cereal, for example, we can let them select one variety. We can be sure they will choose whatever they have seen advertised lately, and it will probably be multicolored and contain a prize! If we can't stand this kind of cereal, we might ask them to bring two boxes—one old standby like Corn Flakes or Rice Crispies that we enjoy and one kind that they prefer!

Another helpful tactic is to allow our children to pick out one toy, one piece of candy, or something special to hold their interest. We can either let them do this early or hold it as a reward for good behavior and let them pick it up at the checkout stand. Although some parents think it is spoiling children to get something every time they go shopping, we need to realize that this is exactly what *we* appear guilty of ourselves. We fill several large bags with things we want and think we spoil our children if we buy them a little piece of candy! Maybe our children deserve the same privilege on a much more limited scale.

Messy Rooms and Chores

As our children grow a little older, we want them to learn to pick up after themselves and maintain at least some semblance of order in their rooms. This is a good and normal expectation. Unfortunately many children do not seem to be born with this desire. The tendency not to pick up after oneself and to leave chores undone is another area that is not necessarily caused by a search for substitute gratification of unmet emotional needs. Generally it is not because they feel unloved and are looking for attention that children fail to pick up their room. And it is not because they are bored and needing excitement that they fail to do their chores. They fail to do these tasks because, like most people, they have a tendency to be lazy. With the exception of workaholics and perfectionists, most of us would prefer not to do our chores if we had the choice. Consequently messy rooms and "forgetting" chores are "normal" reactions.

Many children also have problems with personal hygiene. Children who love to stay clean are clearly in the minority. Most children just will not brush their teeth regularly, wash their faces, and comb their hair without some training or discipline. In deciding to attack any of these problems, we need to avoid two extremes. On the one hand, we should not overact to the tendency to "forget" to do one's chores. Neither should we condemn our children or compare them to their cleaner sister in order to make them feel guilty. This approach undermines our children's developing sense of self-esteem and may cause resentment or rebellion. The other extreme is to act as if there is no problem. Some parents, believing these things should be left up to the children, do very little to help them develop good habits of work and personal hygiene.

The best way to handle these problems is to treat them as entirely normal tendencies while letting our children know we are going to help them develop some good habits. By helping our children plan their schedule of personal and family responsibilities and setting out some clear discipline that will be carried out if they are not done, our children can learn to fulfill these tasks without constant nagging and harassing.

The Need for Order

One of the best ways to avoid conflicts over numerous household tasks is to develop a well-planned schedule of family activities. Left to themselves, children are likely to fuss, dawdle, and forget about a dozen things each morning. They are also likely to either be late for school or go into a panic every morning about three minutes before they should be out the door.

Several years ago we started having this kind of problem in our family. From the time Kathy and I were up and about, we spent most of our time checking on the children's progress. We glanced in their rooms to see if their beds were made. We checked the bathroom to see if they had been there. And we repeatedly asked if they had brushed their teeth, washed their faces, combed their hair, set the table, practiced the piano, and finished a number of other daily duties.

Finally we became tired of the hassle and decided we had better find a workable plan for bringing order into our morning activities. First we established a morning routine. Rather than having them get up around seven, eat sometime between 7:15 and 7:45 and practice piano whenever they could, we developed a daily schedule for both Dickie and Debbie. Everyone was up by 7:00. By 7:30 the pre-breakfast chores were done and one of the children had the table set, so that promptly at 7:30 we sat down for breakfast. At 7:45 one of the children cleared the table while the other practiced piano for fifteen minutes. And in the remaining 15 or 20 minutes before leaving for school, other morning activities were finished.

We also built a little "job box" that held a variety of colored three-by-five cards. Each card had one morning activity printed in bold letters. Dickie and Debbie each had a job box, and each box was divided into two sections. One section was marked TO DO; the other read DONE. Every morning before sitting down for breakfast, each child had to check his or her box and see that all of the pre-breakfast chores were finished. Before they left for school, they had to be sure the remainder were done. This simple little box had a profound effect. It let us stop nagging and helped the children to accept responsibility for their own morning activities. Rather than relying on us to remind them a dozen times, they simply checked their own job boxes.

These simple planning steps helped turn a potentially bad situation into a very good one. Without this kind of order and structure, our children were wandering from one thing to another. They didn't know just when to count on breakfast and then didn't have the help of their job box to remind them of chores undone.

Simple steps like this are an important part of positive parenting. Although we should not develop a rigid program for all our children's activities, they should have help deciding when to carry out their regular responsibilities. This helps to bring order into the family and initiate habits that will serve them well in later life.

Summary

In this chapter we have looked at a few exceptions to the basic premise of this book that children misbehave or have problems because they are trying to fulfill some God-given needs by turning to substitutes or counterfeits. In addition to the problems discussed here, we could include things like wanting to crawl out of a highchair, kicking and squirming when someone is changing a diaper, yelling when someone pulls a comb through your knotted hair or burns your ear with a hair dryer, being cranky when you first wake up in the morning, and a score of others. I stress these exceptions because they make an important difference in the way we choose to discipline and train our children.

If a child leaves his room in a chaotic condition to force us to pay attention because he doesn't feel properly loved and appreciated, we cannot solve this problem by simply telling him he cannot eat breakfast or leave for school until his room is clean. This would not deal with the real problem. In a case like this, we need to pause and ask why this child doesn't feel sufficiently loved and accepted. Then we must take steps to help him fill these needs. In addition to these efforts we might institute some discipline; but to discipline without helping him feel better about himself and his place in the family is a superficial and unsatisfactory solution.

On the other hand, if our child has a messy room simply because of the natural human tendency to put off anything that smacks of work, we do not need to take a great deal of additional time to play with that child and communicate our love to him. We can move right into the training and discipline he needs to learn to accept responsibility.

The same would be true with a teen-ager who is having difficulty carrying out chores like washing the car, mowing the yard, or dusting the living room. Sometimes teen-agers put these chores off because they resent us. Knowing that the failure to do the chores will upset us, they "forget" in order to gain revenge. On other occasions they "forget" because they are in a power struggle: they are not about to let us tell them what to do! But in other cases it is simply a matter of not liking to do any kind of work around the house.

If the problem is a power struggle and we simply tell our teen-agers they are not leaving the house until the work is done, we are likely to stir up even more anger and cause a bigger rift in family unity. At these times we need to evaluate the problem. Do our teen-agers feel that they have to fight us to build up their sense of confidence or strength? Have we been overly protective, critical, or authoritarian? Have we been positive and encouraged them to feel good about themselves and their ideas? Or have we unknowingly undermined their sense of confidence and programed them for this rebellion? If there is a problem here, we need to talk it over with our offspring and get to the root of it before things become worse.[2]

On the other hand, if our children are happy and well-adjusted, but simply don't like to do their chores, we can move right into some discipline that will make sure the chores are done. We can sit down with the children, ask what they think would serve as a good "reminder," reach an agreement, and move ahead.

We can summarize the main points of this chapter as follows:

1. Some of our children's problem behaviors are not caused by unmet emotional needs. They are simply normal reactions that are part of growing up.

2. Some of these reactions (such as an infant not liking certain food or a fidgety child in a market) do not call for corrective discipline. Instead, we as the parents need to make some changes to help our children.

3. Other reactions call for discipline or training. In these cases, however, we should not approach our children as though they were being "bad." We should explain to them (if they are old enough to understand) why something needs to be changed and how we are going to help them.

---

[2]My book *Adolescence Is Not an Illness* (Old Tappan, N.J.: Fleming H. Revell, 1980) deals in depth with this kind of parent-teen problem.

Chapter 10

YOUR CHILD AND ADAM

After a discussion of reasons why children misbehave, a man in the group asked, "But isn't anything just sin? You have given all of these nice reasons why children have problems, but the Bible says our problems come from sin. How does that fit in?"

His question raises an important point. The Bible indeed traces all our problems to our sinful condition. And if we are going to understand our children properly we must come to grips with the influence of sin in their lives. It would be a big mistake to provide a thorough analysis of the psychological causes of our children's actions and consider this a complete explanation. This would be an injustice both to ourselves and our children. We parents would never be able to understand our children's behavior fully, and our children would never learn to accept responsibility for their part in the development of their problems.

On the other hand, simply to label our children's problems "sin" and go on as though that explains everything fails to do justice to the situation. We need to ask questions like "How is sin involved in my children's problems?" or "In what ways is it working?" or "Why did they develop this particular type of problem?"

According to the Bible, sin entered the human race when Adam and Eve decided to take matters into their own hands and become "like God, knowing good and evil" (Gen. 3:5). Their sin was immediately followed by a variety of problems including family squabbles. Adam and Eve were ashamed so they hid themselves (Gen. 3:7). They blamed each other (Gen. 3:11–13). And their children, Cain and Abel, experienced the first case of sibling rivalry—one that ended in murder (Gen. 4:1–10).

Since this beginning, every member of the human race has had to struggle with his or her own sin and the sins of those they live and interact with daily. The effects of sin are seen clearly in at least two ways in family living. To begin with, since Adam and Eve's sin there have been no perfect parents. All of us, no matter how loving and well-intentioned, have problems of our own. We periodically have selfish, frustrated, angry, worried, or jealous thoughts and feelings. Consequently we have difficulty meeting our children's basic emotional needs effectively. If we are selfish, we may elevate our own activities above our children and undermine their sense of being loved. If we are critical or demanding, we can undercut our children's need for confidence. If we are anxious and worrisome, our children are likely to take up our anxiety and have difficulty developing a healthy sense of confidence. And if we have problems with our tempers and tend to yell at our children, condemn, nag, or pressure them, we may undercut their need for a sense of significance and worth. In short, the sin in our own lives is communicated to our children through our failure to fulfill their God-given needs.

This is only one side of the coin, however. According to the Bible, children would have problems even if we were perfect parents! Adam and Eve couldn't blame their problems on their parents: they had to accept the full responsibility. While we are not in the same position as Adam and Eve, there is a lesson there for us. The Bible says that we share a joint responsibility with our children for their development. Proverbs 22:6 instructs us to "Train a child in the way he should go" and promises that if we do "he will not turn from it." Samuel gives us a clear illustration of a father who failed to rear his children properly (1 Sam. 2:12–22). And Moses tells us that the sins of the fathers are passed to the third and fourth generations (Deut. 5:9–10).

But the Bible also tells us, "Even a child is known by his actions" (Prov. 20:11). It instructs children to follow their parents' directions (Eph. 6:1). The Bible leaves no room to blame all of a child's problems on the parents. But neither does it give us room to blame them all on the child.

Who's to Blame?

Without trying to fix blame, but simply to understand, let's look at how our children's sinful tendencies influence their adjustment and behavior.

One very important way sin enters into our children's actions is through the very emotional needs we have been discussing. Beginning with Adam and Eve, none of us has been satisfied to have our needs met solely in the way God intended. The essence of Adam and Eve's sin was that they were not satisfied to find their sense of confidence and worth through their position as bearers of the image of God who were assigned the task of ruling over the earth (Gen. 1:26–31). Rather than gaining satisfaction from being in God's image and having fellowship with Him, they wanted to be gods. They wanted *all* the knowledge God possessed, and they wanted to get it in their own way. In short, they rejected their position as created children whose Parent would adequately supply their needs, and they took it upon themselves to try to fill their needs in their own way.

When our children turn from their God-given needs for love, confidence, worth, and activity to the substitutes of attention, power, perfection, and destructive activity, they are doing precisely the same thing as Adam and Eve. They are saying, "Since I do not believe my needs are being met to my satisfaction, I will take it upon myself to do it my way!" They are rejecting a God-ordained way of having their needs met and are following Satan's substitute. Their needs are legitimate, but the way they attempt to fulfill them is not.

There is, however, a major difference between our children's attempts to meet their God-given needs and Adam and Eve's attempt. Adam and Eve's needs were being perfectly met by their parent, God. But our children are living with less-than-perfect parents who do not fully supply their needs. Our children face a double dilemma. They really do have unmet needs, and if we do not fulfill them, they must search for substitutes. This is where joint responsibility enters in. We cannot, for example, really place the responsibility for our children's attention-getting misbehavior on them if we have not been meeting their needs for love.

Let's say, for example, that God placed Adam and Eve in the Garden, created them with a necessity to eat in order to survive, placed only one source of food in the Garden (the tree of the knowledge of good and evil), and commanded them not to eat or they would die. This would obviously be unfair. Adam and Even would know they had to eat to survive; but there would be no way of meeting their God-given need for food without sinning! Yet this is precisely what many of us do with our children. We busy ourselves with a hundred other things so that our children feel left out and ignored. Then, when they get into trouble to force us to give them attention, we blame them for their problems!

I have seen this same principle operate with a number of teen-age girls who became promiscuous. Their fathers were excessively busy or for some other reason were unable to build warm, loving relationships with their daughters. At the same time their mothers did not feel very good about themselves or their role as women, so they were unable to help their daughters develop a healthy sense of confidence in their ability to relate to the opposite sex. Searching for the love they didn't receive from their fathers and the confidence in their femininity that they didn't learn from their mothers, they turned to premarital sex. Their promiscuity was a substitute for God-given needs that were not met.

Now, certainly these girls must assume a good deal of responsibility for their behavior. But it is also obvious that the parents' inability to meet their daughters' needs was a strong motivating force behind their promiscuity. There was an interaction of personal and parental responsibility in these adolescents' misguided search to meet their God-given needs in unhealthy and sinful ways. Similarly, children who have been criticized, repeatedly compared with siblings, or brought up by rather rigid or stubborn parents cannot be blamed entirely for their stubborn, power-oriented lifestyle. Given their family environment, this is the only way they know to cope.

Everyone Wants to Be Number One

Along with their attempts to meet their needs for love, confidence, worth, and activity, all persons since Adam and Eve have had another problem. We have not been content simply with being loved: we have wanted to be loved more than anyone else. We have not been content with being average, healthy, competent people: we have wanted to be the most competent or powerful. We haven't been satisfied with just a healthy sense of worth: we have wanted to be better or more important than everyone else. And we haven't been content to busy ourselves simply with what God intended: we have wanted to do whatever we please.

Let's consider our children's need for love, for example. If we have more than one child, we have no doubt noticed that there is a great deal of competition for our love and acceptance. Although they know better intellectually, all our children would like to be number one in our love. I remember how, when our children were still very young, Dickie popped into my lap one day and asked, "Daddy, do you love me?"

"I do," I replied, giving him a big hug.

"How much?" Dickie queried.

"As much as any father has ever loved a son, Dickie," I answered, looking him straight in the eye.

"Really?" Dickie responded with a big smile.

"Really!" I replied. Then, with a mischievous look on his face, he asked, "More than Debbie?"

I thought fast and answered, "Dickie, you are our first child and our son, and I have a very special love for you!"

"Really!" he responded and lit up again.

"Really!" I replied.

Then he asked again, "More than Debbie?"

"Dickie," I replied, "Debbie is our second child and our daughter, and I have a very special kind of love for her."

"Oh," he said, as a discouraged look spread over his face.

Our conversation went round and round, with Dickie trying every way he knew to con me into telling him I loved him more than Debbie! All my assurance that I loved him with all the love I had, that I loved him with a special love, and that I didn't love anyone more than him wouldn't really satisfy him. He wanted to be number one! All children have similar desires, and these desires stem directly from Adam's sin. Since that time, every person wants to be number one in many aspects of life.

The same is true about our children's search for confidence. Think of how hard your children compete to win in football, soccer, gym, and other contests. They try their best, become deeply involved, and feel either terrible or terrific, depending on the outcome. If they win, they run off the field excitedly with a certain air of confidence. But if they lose, they walk slowly off the field with a look of defeat and dejection. They either blame themselves and feel depressed or turn their shattered feelings on the umpire, the referee, the "dirty play," or the "big guy" on the other team. Few children are satisfied just to compete for the fun of it; they want to win because they want to be better. They want to build up their confidence at the expense of others.

The same is true in grades, band, cheerleading, and chorus tryouts. While not every child competes in every field, most children try to find one or more areas where they can be "the best." In fact, have you noticed that children in the same family often tend to find their identity in different activities so they won't have to compete head to head with their brothers and sisters? If our first child is a gifted athlete, our second might become a serious student and the third a socialite. They try to choose activities in which they can successfully perform and "be the best"—at least in their own family!

This is not all bad. It is good to do our best. But this points

up some implications of competition. In every match there is
a winner and a loser. The winner earns good feelings about
himself by defeating the loser—not simply by doing his best.
The Bible tells us, "Let everyone be sure that he is doing his
very best, for then he will have the personal satisfaction of
work well done, and won't need to compare himself with
someone else (Gal. 6:4 LIVING BIBLE).

At home the desire to be the most competent often shows
up in putting down one's brothers and sisters. While sibling
conflicts are accentuated by parental favoritism, criticism,
lack of clearly communicated love, and unwise comparisons,
these are not the sole causes. Even in loving homes with
sensitive parents, there will be some sibling fights. These
fights are motivated by the desire to be either the most loved
or the most competent. In putting a sibling down, our sons
and daughters are attempting to elevate themselves.

The delicate interaction of our children's own desires to
fulfill their emotional needs in godlike fashion and our parental responsibility for successfully meeting their God-given
needs for love, confidence, and worth call for a great deal of
sensitivity on our part. Most of us are prone to go to one of
two extremes. Either we assume all the responsibility ourselves, or we blame our children.

If we take all the responsibility, we attribute all our children's problems to our ineffectiveness as parents and end up
feeling guilty and depressed. On the other hand, if we tend to
blame our children, we say things like "I love my children
plenty. If they are fighting, it is their own problem. You
surely can't blame me for their sibling fights. Besides, all kids
fight."

Both perspectives miss the point. If we are to do the best
job possible, we must become sensitive both to our children's
excessive demands for power, confidence, and love and to our
difficulty in communicating our love and building up their
sense of confidence and worth. We must learn to tell the
difference between sibling fights growing out of our own lack

of attention to our children or their boredom and those growing out of their wish to have everyone in the world at their
beck and call. The key to this is our own sensitivity. If we
really listen, most of us can tell whether our children are
misbehaving because of some inner frustration and need or
because of an emotionally strong but selfish desire.

The ability to tell the difference between these two kinds of
misbehavior has some important implications. If our children's misbehavior is motivated by unmet needs, the solution
lies not in corrective discipline like sending our children to
their rooms or grounding them, but rather in taking steps to
increase their level of self-confidence, worth, and feelings of
belongingness. On the other hand, if our children's needs
have been well met and they are misbehaving in order to have
their way in everything, control the family, or be the center of
attention, they need corrective discipline. As we saw earlier,
it is unfair to attempt to discipline children for actions growing
out of our lack of success in helping them to fill their needs.
But to fail to correct and discipline children for misbehavior
motivated by selfish desires for control and attention is
equally unhelpful and ultimately unfair to them.

The following questions can help us differentiate between
children who are misbehaving because they want to be number
one and those who are motivated by a search to find substitutes
for unmet needs. None of these guidelines can give an absolute
answer, but taken together they can shed much light on the
causes of our children's adjustment problems.

*Have we done anything today to help our children feel
loved, accepted, and an integral part of our family?* This is
one of the easiest ways to get a fix on our children's emotional
situation. Every child needs some time every day when he or
she has a parent's complete attention. Every child needs a
chance to be listened to without interruption, to be understood, and to have our love and interest clearly communicated. Sometimes we can do this in a couple of minutes in the
morning, and sometimes it may take being together an hour

or more. But however we do it, we must be sure our children daily hear the message that we love them. If they are hearing this regularly and still resort to attention-getting devices, this is more likely due to excessive demands rather than an unmet need for love.

Has anything happened in the last few days that would undermine our children's confidence? Losing an important contest, receiving a driving ticket, having an accident, or any number of situations may seriously undermine our children's confidence. Sometimes their fussy and temperamental moods can be traced directly to this kind of problem. If so, we need to help bridge these gaps and restore their confidence so they can move ahead.

Have our children been active in constructive, interesting activities? If our children's schedules have become routine and boring and they have had little to do, they are very likely to get into trouble to let us know they have a legitimate need. They are not trying to misbehave for misbehavior's sake, and they are not trying to be rebellious. They are simply giving us a message that they need our help.

How are our children getting along with their friends? Jealousy, conflicts, and rejection by peers can seriously undermine our psychic balance, especially during adolescence. Before we assume our children are misbehaving merely because of their negative or sinful attitudes, we should look at their life situation. Very often an understanding of what is going on with their friends will show that our offspring need our help through some very difficult struggles and not correction for bad attitudes.

Are our children feeling good about themselves? When our children have basically positive feelings about themselves but are acting up, it is more likely to be due to their own sinful tendencies than to our failure to supply their God-given needs. We need to look carefully to see that they are not feeling inferior and do not have a false (compensatory) sense of superiority. If they are not, we can proceed with appropriate discipline or correction. If they are, we will need to back up and attend to these needs.

Is our family atmosphere generally happy and cooperative with only sporadic problems? Some homes are in chaos from morning to night. This usually reflects either our inability to provide well for our children's emotional needs or our inability to discipline effectively and consistently. Other families run basically well, and the children are generally content. When the latter is true, it is more likely that our children's occasional problems can be chalked up to their own sinful propensities than to our failure to provide adequately for their needs.

Chapter 11

WHAT DO WE DO NOW?

Let's summarize what we have said so far and consider how we can be sure we understand our children's needs and know where to go from there.

God creates every child with a number of emotional and physical needs and gives parents the primary responsibility for seeing that those needs are met through adolescence. In our society, most of our children's physical needs are easily cared for. Their emotional needs, however, are much more complex and difficult to fill. When our children's needs for love, confidence, worth, and constructive activity are met, family life is fairly peaceful. Being happy and contented, our children have a minimum of conflicts and problems of adjustment. But when our children feel unloved, incompetent, unworthy, or bored, they are destined for trouble. They seek out situations that enable them to find temporary substitutes for their God-given needs. Unfortunately these substitute activities nearly always result in conflicts, problems, and misbehavior. Table I summarizes these basic needs and their substitutes.

Table I

Basic Needs and Substitutes

God-given need	Child's feeling when need is not met	Substitute
Love	Lonely, isolated, depressed	Attention
Confidence	Weak, helpless, inferior	Power and control
Worth	Worthless, useless, no good	Perfectionism and performance
Constructive activity	Bored, restless	(Destructive) Activity

Each of our children's God-given needs has a rather specific and predictable substitute or counterfeit. The substitute for confidence is power and control. The substitute for worth is perfectionism and performance. The substitute for constructive activity is destructive activity. Besides these specific substitute motivations, however, there are two other important motivating forces behind our children's misbehavior. These are psychological safety and revenge.

The first four substitutes relate to only one specific need: attention, for example, is a substitute for love and not for power or worth. But psychological safety and revenge can come into play when any of our four basic needs are not met. If our children feel unloved, they may retreat to some form of behavior designed to ensure their psychological safety, or they may become angry and try to get even with us in addition to turning to attention-getting behavior. Similarly, if their confidence is undermined, they may either withdraw (a search for psychological safety) or fight back (to gain revenge) along with looking for power or control. The same is true when the children feel unworthy or bored: besides turning to the substitute, they may also seek revenge or psychological safety. We can diagram the sequence of activities that leads up to our children's misbehavior this way:

God-given need (if not met) → feelings of

{ loneliness
depression
inferiority
helplessness
worthlessness
boredom }

↗ search for Substitutes

{ attention
power & control
perfectionism &
performance
substitute activity }

+ search for psychological
safety or revenge

Apart from these motives for misbehavior there exists much seeming misbehavior that is entirely normal. Such action is a product of either a normal developmental level or an inherited temperament. In these cases we need to be careful not to attach a moral judgment to our children's activities, but learn instead to cope with these stages and channel their energy and their temperament styles in positive directions.

With this foundation, we are now in a position to understand the causes of our children's misbehavior and attack underlying problems rather than surface manifestations. When we reach this point, we have taken a great stride toward effective parenting. We can move beyond a symptom approach and start to focus on the real source of our children's problems—their emotional needs and their sinful propensities.

Although a symptom approach may enable us to force our children temporarily to behave the way we want, it does so at the expense of their inner emotional and spiritual health. The Bible says, "Out of the overflow of the heart the mouth speaks" (Matt. 12:34). God's first concern is our inner attitudes and feelings. When these are in good shape, healthy behavior naturally follows. This is as true of children as of adults. No amount of forcing, pressuring, or molding our children's actions is sufficient to rear mature people; we must first learn to be sensitive to their basic God-given needs and find ways of fulfilling them.

This approach initially takes a little time and effort. But with practice we can learn to be sensitive to the needs and feelings that lie beneath our children's misbehavior. Once we do, we are in a much better position to discipline and train effectively.

By now you may be feeling, "But I am not a psychologist. I cannot take all day to analyze the hidden, esoteric reasons why my children act as they do. It is much easier simply to threaten or punish them if they don't shape up!" I understand your feelings: I sometimes feel the same way! But fortunately the causes of our children's misbehavior are not terribly complex and esoteric. Once we learn a few principles, we can readily and effectively size up the situation and plan appropriate action. In fact, we as parents are probably much better judges of what is going on in our children's psychic life than most psychologists. All we need to do is to learn to listen for a few keys or guideposts that point almost without error to the causes of our children's conflicts and frustrations. Tables II, III, and IV spell out these guides.[1]

Table II
Our Child's Behavior

if our child's motivation is . . . he will probably be	
Attention	Noisy, restless, a showoff, and getting into situations that guarantee that we will stop what we are doing and focus on him.
Power and control	Aggressive, defiant toward authority, insolent, and will refuse to do his work, disobey, try to be the boss, and pout and sulk when he cannot have his way. May also use passive control methods.
Perfectionism and performance	Extremely polite and cooperative. A good student who tries very hard to please. May also show signs of pressure and disappointment when he cannot be the best.
Destructive activity	Bored, restless, goes from one thing to another, frequently interrupts and asks "What can I do?" or gets into some mischievous or destructive activity.
Revenge	Verbally or physically assaultive or hurtful, teasing.
Psychological safety	Avoiding situations and feelings that are potentially threatening, or trying to ensure his innocence or safety. May give up and stop trying.

[1]The format of these three guides is adapted from *Winning Over Children* by Francis X. Walton and Robert L. Powers (Chicago: Practical Psychology Assoc., 1974). Used by permission.

Table III
Our Child's Response to Discipline

If our child's motivation is . . .	he will probably respond to correction by
Attention	Stopping for a short time (because he received more attention) but then beginning again (since he is looking for more).
Power and control	Continuing to fight in some way. He may get worse, threaten retaliation, or find a passive means of control.
Perfectionism and performance	Trying harder, becoming discouraged, or feeling he can't please.
Destructive activity	Feeling misunderstood, becoming discouraged, or continuing to seek for some way to break the boredom.
Revenge	Talking back, becoming worse, or seeking other means of retaliating.
Psychological safety	Increasing his use of the mechanisms already in use.

Table IV
Our Reaction to Our Child's Misbehavior

If your child's motivation is . . .	we will probably feel
Attention	Annoyed and tend to think of our child as a pest or a bother. He is in the way or disturbing us.
Power and control	Angry, challenged, or defeated. We will want to fight back to prove we are the boss, or give up and quit.
Perfectionism	Pride in our child but wonder if he is "too good." We may be concerned about his inability to relax, take it easy, or not always be "the winner."
Destructive activity	Bothered and want to be left alone. We think they should find ways of taking care of themselves.

| Revenge | Angry or, if the child is older, hurt. How could they treat us this way after all we have done for them? |
| Psychological safety | Frustrated because we don't know how to reach our child. Other reactions vary with our child's defense. In withdrawal we may feel like giving up or be very worried. In rationalization we may become angry. |

We can see that both our children's behavior and our reaction to it usually give a clear answer to what is motivating a misbehavior. Once we learn the meaning of each kind of misbehavior, we are well on the way to solving our children's adjustment problems. We can start to help them meet their basic God-given needs, and we can see that we don't unknowingly reinforce their substitute goals.

Let us consider attention-getting children as an example. They are repeatedly getting into fights with their brother, acting smart in public, throwing a tantrum, or in some way calling attention to themselves. As soon as we realize what is happening, we can stop rewarding their attention-seeking behavior. We can ignore the tantrum, let them work out their own problems with their brother, and stop laughing at their smart-aleck comments or stop reprimanding them.[2] This ignoring in itself will start to lessen the problem. If we are going to be fully effective, however, we must also help our children see what they are trying to do and offer better ways of expressing their needs.

We may ask them, "Billy, do you know why you keep picking on your brother?" Billy very likely will say no. Then we can sensitively say, "I wonder if it is because you want mommy to spend more time with you?" or "I wonder if it's because you think mommy spends too much time with Johnnie?" or "I wonder if it's because you want mother to pay more attention to you?"

---

[2]Chapter 4 of *Help! I'm a Parent* goes into more depth in handling temper tantrums.

When we get close to the truth, we will usually see a little smile or some form of recognition. Our children know that we understand their hidden message, and they are feeling better already! When both the children and we parents understand what the misbehavior is trying to accomplish, we can set about finding better ways of achieving the goal. As parents we can find more time for each child, plan some special times alone, take more time to ask about the day's activities, show more physical affection, and communicate our love in a variety of ways. We can also let the child know there are better ways of telling us when he or she is feeling left out, lonely, inadequate, or bored.

When my children were very young, they learned to come to us and say, "Daddy (or Mommy), I need a little more attention." You can't believe how rewarding it is to see your child come up with a questioning smile and tell you his needs like that! You can sense his trust in you, his knowledge that you really want his best, and his assurance that if he tells you what he needs you will do your best to help. You also know that in his coming to you he has probably chosen not to try to gain attention by beating on his sister or some other unacceptable means.

If we sense that our children's misbehavior is motivated by the search for power or control, we might say something like "It seems as if you really want your way!" or "You really don't want anyone telling you what to do, do you?" or "It seems as if you really want to show dad you're the boss!" Once again, when we see the sign of recognition, we will know we are on the right track.

If the problem is rooted in our children's search for psychological safety, we can say something like "It really seems scary out there, doesn't it?" or "It's really hard to be wrong, isn't it?" or "You must not feel too happy down inside." All these comments are designed to get into our children's shoes and let them know we understand that they don't feel safe and that their behavior makes sense to us. Then we can encourage them to tell us more about how they are. The more we understand their frightening inner world, the better we can help them to develop confidence and skills they need to give up their maladaptive safety measures.

In each case our goal is to become our children's friend or ally. Rather than being the ogre standing by to discipline every time children misbehave, we are learning to be encouraging parents. This is one of the key ingredients of positive parenting. Although there is plenty of room for discipline, we are letting our children know that our primary concern is with their happiness. We are trying first to fulfill their needs. Then, after we have fulfilled this God-given responsibility, we will carry out any discipline that is needed.

Since this book is aimed largely at prevention, we do not have the time to go into the specifics of corrective discipline. My book *Help! I'm a Parent* is written for that very purpose. It begins at this point, where we have begun to understand our children's needs and see how we can meet them. It discusses what to do *after* we have identified the problem and begun to help our children meet their needs for love, confidence, constructive activity, and worth. Identification of the problem and meeting the needs are the foundations of all good parenting. But we also need to know how to discipline children with problems like messy rooms, sibling fights, mealtime and homework hassles, temper tantrums, curfew violations, and other daily problems. *Help! I'm a Parent* addresses these and other matters of practical discipline. These two books are written to be used together—*Why Children Misbehave*, to understand our children's needs and how we can more effectively fulfill them in order to avoid as much misbehavior as possible—and *Help! I'm a Parent*, to see what we can do after our children misbehave. If you want to go beyond an understanding of ways of meeting your children's needs, to specific ways of disciplining and correcting children, *Help! I'm a Parent* can help you do that.